Iris Szaszi, Rudolf Szaszi

Get Well

Berufliches Englisch für
Gesundheits- und Pflegeberufe

6. Auflage

Bestellnummer 10657

■ Bildungsverlag EINS
westermann

Bildquellenverzeichnis
Fotolia: Cover (Kzenon), 9.1 (Daniel Fleck), 16.1 (CandyBox), 16.2 (CandyBox), 16.3 (CandyBox), 17.1 (Deklofenak), 19.1 (Monkey Business), 19.2 (Deklofenak), 19.3 (FikMik), 22.1 (contrastwerkstatt), 23.1 (Kadmy), 25.1 (Sergey Galushko), 25.2 (Kadmy), 39.2 (psdesign1), 43.1 (lexaarts), 55.1 (andilevkin), 64.1 (Sergey Kohl), 64.2 (Fotowerk), 72.1 (Yuri Arcurs), 75.1 (Vladimir Badaev), 75.2 (CandyBox Images), 76.1 (Vladimir Andruschenko), 79.4 (Daniel Fleck), 79.5 (Daniel Fleck), 81.1 (Daniel Fleck), 82.1 (Jürgen Fälchle), 85.1 (vgstudio), 85.2 (Imagery Majestic), 93.1 (daboost), 95.1 (Kaarsten), 97.1 (samott), 99.1 (sborisov)
Iris und Rudolf Szaszi: 5.1, 10.1, 13.1, 14.1, 14.2, 14.3, 17.2, 18.1, 18.2, 20.1, 20.2, 21.1, 21.2, 27.1, 27.2, 27.3, 27.4, 27.5, 27.6, 27.7, 27.8, 27.9, 28.1, 29.1, 30.1, 42.1, 46.1, 46.2, 46.3, 48.1, 52.1, 66.1, 67.1, 78.1, 87.1, 96.1, 96.2

Zeichnungen:
Angelika Brauner/BV1, Köln: 41.1, 37.1, 40.1
Elisabeth Gallas/BV1, Köln: 79.1, 79.2, 79.3
Cornelia Kurtz/ BV1, Köln: 15.1, 71.1, 77.1, 81.2, 81.3, 81.4
Jörg Mair/BV1, Köln: 39.1

service@bv-1.de
www.bildungsverlag1.de

Bildungsverlag EINS GmbH
Ettore-Bugatti-Straße 6-14, 51149 Köln

ISBN 978-3-427-10657-9

westermann GRUPPE

Vorwort

Get Well - Berufliches Englisch für Gesundheits- und Pflegeberufe ist ein erfahrungs- und handlungsorientiertes Lehrwerk. Es richtet sich an angehende Medizinische Fachangestellte, Tiermedizinische Fachangestellte, Zahnmedizinische Fachangestellte, Pharmazeutisch-kaufmännische Angestellte, Pflegeassistentinnen und Pflegeassistenten sowie Altenpflegerinnen und Altenpfleger, die im Rahmen des berufsbildenden Unterrichts berufsbezogenes Englisch lernen.

Es kann aber ebenso für bereits im Beruf tätige Mitarbeiterinnen und Mitarbeiter interessant sein, die ihre Englischkenntnisse sowie das spezifische Fachvokabular ihres Berufes
auffrischen und sich mittels des Internets englischsprachige Informationen zu ihrem Berufsfeld beschaffen möchten.
Außerdem kann das Lehrbuch für diejenigen Personen hilfreich sein, die berufliches Englisch außerhalb Deutschlands anwenden.

Das Lehrwerk richtet sich an Personen, deren Englischkenntnisse dem Niveau eines Sekundarabschlusses 1 entsprechen. Es werden keine Kenntnisse des Fachvokabulars Gesundheit und Altenpflege vorausgesetzt.

In erster Linie zielt das Buch auf die sprachlich angemessene Betreuung englisch-sprachiger Patientinnen und Patienten in der Praxis, englischsprachiger Kundinnen und Kunden in der Apotheke sowie englischsprachiger Bewohnerinnen und Bewohner im Altenheim.
Zur Förderung der Kommunikation werden Fachausdrücke und Redemittel für praxisorientierte Dialoge und Rollenspiele zur Verfügung gestellt. Grundlegende grammatikalische Strukturen werden wiederholt und geübt.

Durch die Erstellung von Handlungsprodukten, die die Suche nach Informationen im Internet, deren Auswahl, sprachliche und visuelle Aufbereitung sowie Präsentation beinhaltet, sollen Schlüsselqualifikationen gefördert werden, wie die selbstständige Erschließung von Fachinhalten, aber insbesondere zielgerichtete Teamarbeit. Kooperatives Lernen und Arbeiten hat hohe Relevanz im Hinblick auf die veränderten Anforderungen in den Arbeitsfeldern Gesundheit und Altenpflege.

Die zielgerichtete Internetrecherche sowie der im Lehrwerk gestaltete Wechsel im Hinblick auf Methoden und Sozialformen soll eine hohe Schüleraktivität intendieren, im Rahmen derer die Lehrkraft zum Moderator von Lernprozessen wird. Zum Erfassen der authentischen Texte aus dem Internet können zweisprachige Wörterbücher zur Verfügung gestellt werden bzw. ein Online-Wörterbuch verwendet werden.

Nach Möglichkeit sollte fächer- und lernfeldübergreifend in Absprache mit Kolleginnen und Kollegen gearbeitet werden.

Iris und Rudolf Szaszi

Contents

Who are you?

1.1 Getting to know each other in class

Warming up

Say your name and something you like which has to begin with the same letter as your forename:

I am **T**anja and I like **t**eddy-bears. This is **T**anja and she likes **t**eddy-bears, I am **S**teffi and I like **s**hopping.

Each student has to repeat names and likes of the ones before and adds her name and like.

Please pay attention in order to get to know each other.

Presentation task

Please write your name onto a piece of paper. The teacher collects all papers, mixes and distributes them. You get a piece of paper with a name you do not know, walk around the classroom and try to find the person whose name you've got.
Ask your partner some questions and then introduce her/him to the class. Find out what she/he likes and doesn't like (for example TV programmes, cinema films, books, pets, music, holidays …).
Note the most important information you need to introduce your partner on a piece of paper.

This is _____ .

She/he is _____ years old.

She/he comes from _____ .

She/he works at_____ .

She/he likes _____ .

She/he doesn't like_____ .

1.2 Holiday Talk

Tom:	Hello. Nice to meet you. My name's Tom.
Karina:	*Hello. I'm Karina. And this is Wiebke.*
Frank:	Nice to see you. I'm Frank. Tom and I come from Denver.
Wiebke:	*Great. I always wanted to travel to the United States.*
Frank:	Oh, I love Portugal – the wonderful beach, the friendly people, the girls …
Tom:	That's right. Life in Denver is very hectic, especially at Western State College.
Frank:	Where do you come from?

Karina:	*We're from Germany.*
Frank:	Do you go to college or have you got a job in Germany?
Karina:	*A year ago I began a vocational training as a doctor's assistant.*
Tom:	And what about you, Wiebke?
Wiebke:	*I have been an apprentice since last year. I work at a dental surgery in Wilhelmshaven.*
Frank:	And do you like your work?
Karina:	*Well, it depends. The doctor is easy to work with and our surgery is very comfortable. But you must be able to work under pressure. Patients expect you to be cheerful and understanding all the time.*
Wiebke:	*That's true. You really have to be open-minded and a good listener. And not only patients have their expectations. My boss and the colleagues want me to be responsible and well-organized. Nowadays you must be able to work in a team, you see.*
Tom:	Really?
Karina:	*Yes, of course. And also think about new technologies. We have computerized records and scheduling. I work in a high-quality surgery where computer software knowledge and communication skills are a must.*
Frank:	Mmm, possibly. I personally thought that medical assistants just answer the phone, give appointments or assist during treatments.
Tom:	I think most people believe that.
Karina:	*That's a pity. I think we have qualified jobs and we like the work. Oh, by the way, would you like to come to a party tonight?*
Tom:	Yes, we'd love to.
Wiebke:	*It's in Albufeira at the KISS disco.*
Tom:	Okay, see you. Have a nice day.
Karina:	*You too. See you later.*

Make a list of key qualifications which are mentioned in the talk and give the German equivalents.

1.3 Internet Research

Imagine you were Karina. Back home in Germany you want to get information about Denver, the college Frank and Tom attend and about health in Denver. Make an internet research together with a partner.

Use **www.google.com**

Print out a page you find interesting for the class and present what you have found.

Grammar Revision

Present Tense

Present Tense wird verwendet, wenn etwas *regelmäßig* und *wiederholt* geschieht sowie bei *Gewohnheiten.*

Present Tense of:

ich bin: _____ du bist: _____ er ist: _____ sie ist: _____ es ist: _____

wir sind: _____ ihr seid: _____ sie sind: _____

Please translate:

1. Er ist nicht reich. _____

2. Ist sie glücklich? _____

3. Wir sind 5 Medizinische Fachangestellte. _____

4. Ich bin Zahnmedizinische Fachangestellte. _____

5. Ich gehe jeden Samstag in die Disco. _____

6. Du kaufst immer guten Kaffee. _____

Wie werden bei der 3. Person Singular (he, she, it) die Verben verändert?

Please fill in the correct form of the verbs:

1. I go – he _____ 2. I do – he _____

3. I watch – she _____ 4. I carry – she _____

5. I try – he _____ 6. I play – she _____

7. I have – he _____

The Possessive Pronouns (Die besitzanzeigenden Fürwörter)

Please fill in the correct possessive pronouns:

This is _____ surgery. (meine Praxis) This is _____ surgery. (unsere Praxis)

This is _____ surgery. (deine Praxis) This is _____ surgery. (eure Praxis)

This is _____ surgery. (seine Praxis) This is _____ surgery. (ihre Praxis)

This is _____ surgery. (ihre Praxis)

Translate the following sentences:

Dies ist mein Auto. _____

Er mag seine Freundin. _____

Euer Kind ist müde. _____

Diana tanzt mit ihrem Freund. _____

Sie können Ihre Bücher nicht finden. _____

Ist dies Ihre Telefonnummer? _____

Unsere Patienten sind freundlich. _____

Present Continuous

Present Continuous wird verwendet, wenn es um *Handlungen* geht, die *während des Sprechens im Verlauf* sind oder in der *nahen Zukunft* stattfinden werden.

Signalwörter: just, at the moment, right now, look, listen, tonight ...

Das Present Continuous wird gebildet aus einer Form von *to be + ing:*

Please complete:

Ich sehe mir gerade ein Video an: I'm watching a video at the moment.

Du siehst dir gerade ein Video an: _____

Er sieht sich gerade ein Video an: _____

Sie sieht sich gerade ein Video an: _____

Wir sehen uns gerade ein Video an: _____

Ihr seht euch gerade ein Video an: _____

Sie sehen sich gerade ein Video an: _____

Please translate:

1. Ich schlafe im Moment nicht.   _____

2. Er sitzt gerade nicht vor dem Computer. _____

3. Schreibt er jetzt einen Liebesbrief? _____

Complete the sentences with the correct form of the verb in brackets:

1. Martina usually _____ (to drink) coffee, but today she _____ (to drink) tea.

2. Some people _____ (to watch) TV every morning.

3. I _____ (to listen) to the radio at the moment.

4. Look! She _____ (to wash) her hands now.

5. It often _____ (to rain) in Germany,

   but it never _____ (to rain) in Southern California.

6. Mandy always _____ (to finish) work at four o'clock.

Where do you work?

2.1 We all care for your health

Please fill in the German terms

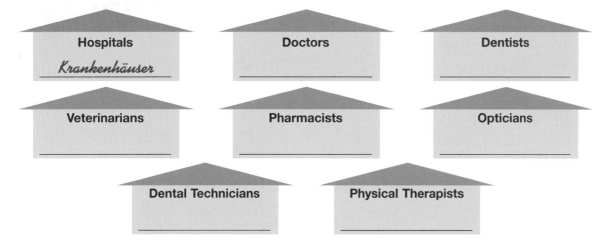

Hospitals	Doctors	Dentists
Krankenhäuser		

Veterinarians	Pharmacists	Opticians

Dental Technicians	Physical Therapists

Fach- und Zusatzbezeichnungen in der Medizin

Zahnarzt	dentist	**Augenarzt**	ophthalmologist
Frauenarzt	gynaecologist	**Allgemeinmediziner**	general practitioner
Kinderarzt	paediatrician	**Kardiologe**	cardiologist
Nervenarzt	neurologist	**Hämatologe**	haematologist
Urologe	urologist	**Gastroenterologe**	gastroenterologist
Chirurg	surgeon	**Hautarzt**	dermatologist
Tierarzt	veterinarian	**Radiologe**	radiologist
Orthopäde	orthopaedist	**Hals-Nasen-Ohren-Arzt**	ENT specialist (ear, nose and throat specialist)

Where do you work?

I work for a _____

_____

There are many different kinds of doctors:
What are doctors called who . . .?

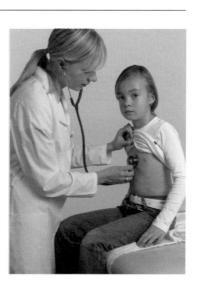

1. repair broken bones _____

2. examine your blood _____

3. take X-rays (pictures of what is inside you) _____

4. do operations _____

5. examine children _____

6. examine your skin _____

7. treat diseases of women _____

8. treat your eyes,
   prescribe glasses
   and contact lenses   _____

9. examine the bladder
   and the kidneys   _____

10. treat your ear, your
    nose and your throat   _____

11. examine your stomach
    and your intestines   _____

12. are heart specialists   _____

13. are not specialized   _____

14. are specialized
    in the nervous system   _____

15. examine teeth   _____

16. treat animals   _____

2.2 My job as a doctor's assistant

The following signs should show you what kind of rooms we have in our surgery, but someone has removed the English terms.

Please fill in the English terms.

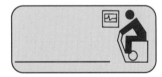

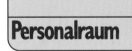

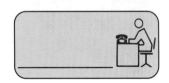

★ **Reception:**
Here you can find the telephone, the computer, file card boxes and the time schedule.

★ **Laboratory:**
In this room we check blood and urine.

★ **Staff cloakroom:**
This room has personal lockers and facilities for hanging clothes (for example our white coats).

★ **Electrocardiography:**
Patients who have problems with their heart get a special examination in this room.

★ **X-ray-room / No admittance:**
In this room we put a lead apron on the patient and process X-rays.

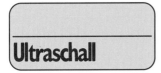

Ultraschall

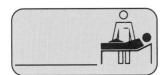

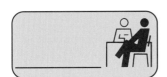

★ **Treatment room:**

In this room the examination couch is located. Here the doctor measures blood pressure, weighs patients and does general examinations.

★ **Consulting room:**

In this room the doctor talks to patients and gives them prescriptions.

★ **Waiting-room:**

In this room the patients can relax before the examination begins.

★ **Ultrasound:**

In this room you find a machine which works with sound waves beyond the frequencies that human beings can hear. (Bats, for example, can hear them.)

Silvia Klein
Lavesstr. 9
30159 Hannover
Germany

Dear Marcia,

Thank you for your letter and the nice photo of your family.
I would really like to visit you and spend three weeks in San Francisco.
Although you invited me to stay at your place, I'll have to save money for the flight.
As you know, I started a vocational training as a doctor's assistant two months ago.
I work at a gynaecological surgery.
My boss and my colleagues are very friendly and explain everything very patiently.
I usually arrive at 7.30 and clean the two treatment rooms. The washbasins have to be disinfected and the sterile instruments have to be sorted into the correct drawers.
The first appointment is at 8.00. I take each patient to the treatment room and do office work. This means I have to give appointments to the patients who ring up, and to write letters. From time to time, I tidy up the waiting-room and talk to patients.
Yesterday, a young woman cried in my arms. She couldn't believe the diagnosis: breast cancer!
It was terrible. How could I help her? I couldn't sleep the whole night.
Sometimes I think I'm too young for this responsibility, and that I can't stand all these problems.
What do you think about my job?
Please tell me what I shall do.

Yours,

Silvia

Individual work: Please answer the questions in complete sentences.

1. Where does Marcia live?

   _____

2. When did Silvia start the vocational training as a doctor's assistant?

   _____

3. Where does Silvia work?

   _____

4. Does Silvia like her boss and her colleagues?

   _____

5. What does Silvia do with the treatment rooms?

   _____

6. What does she do with the washbasins?

   _____

7. What does she do with the sterile instruments?

   _____

8. What kind of office work does Silvia do?

   _____

9. What was the event Silvia was shocked by?

   _____

10. Have you ever experienced a similar event at your surgery?

    _____

11. Imagine you were Marcia. Write a letter to Silvia and tell her what you would advise her to do.

    _____

Individual work: Please ask questions for the underlined parts.

1. Silvia Klein is <u>seventeen</u> years old.

   _____

2. <u>A few weeks ago</u> she left school.

   _____

3. She works <u>at Dr Berg's surgery</u>.

   _____

4. <u>Her boss</u> is very friendly.

   _____

5. She <u>disinfects the washbasins</u>.

   _____

6. A young woman cried, <u>because she couldn't believe the diagnosis</u>.

   _____

Individual work: Please read the following sentences. If the sentence is true, put a T on the line after the sentence. Put an F if the sentence is false, and write the correct sentence on the line.

1. Silvia Klein is nineteen years.

   _____

2. Silvia doesn't want to fly to San Francisco.

_____

3. Her colleagues have no time to explain everything.

_____

4. Silvia must give appointments.

_____

5. She works at a dermatological surgery.

_____

6. She never tidies up the waiting-room.

_____

7. She usually arrives at eight.

_____

Individual work: Please complete the following sentences.

1. A doctor's assistant takes _____ to the treatment room.

2. A doctor's assistant does _____ work.

3. A doctor's assistant sorts the _____ instruments into

the correct _____.

4. A doctor's assistant gives _____ to the patients who ring up.

Pair-work

Try to sketch at least one typical part of your daily routine as a doctor's assistant by either

☐ drawing a cartoon or

☐ writing a poem or

☐ producing a wall-picture or

☐ …

and present your product to your classmates. They may ask questions – so be prepared to give some information about your creative work.

2.3 My job as a veterinarian's assistant

Good morning. Do you know Huntsville Animal Hospital? Probably you don't. Our animal surgery is in Canada, 360 kilometres from Ottawa. My name is Maureen Carter. I have been working here as a veterinarian's assistant for two years.

A typical day in our surgery

Today we had 15 animals in our surgery. First, there was Sissy, a cat who had to be castrated. I handed instruments while my colleague Peggy held her. Sissy got an intravenous injection before the opera-
5 tion began. We always anaesthetize small animals in this way.

Secondly, there was Roger, a rabbit whose teeth had to be shortened. Our boss told his owner to feed him more carrots and lettuce.

10 Thirdly, there was a turtle whom the vet prescribed vitamins in order to give the turtle the chance to survive the cold Canadian winter months.

By the way, there are pet owners who want to know from Peggy and me how to feed their animals, how
15 to bring up their puppies and how to protect them from certain infectious diseases. Although we are just assistants, we have a fair knowledge of all these special things.

Before lunch, Mrs Brown arrived with Jacky, a gol-
20 den retriever who was vaccinated against rabies.
During lunch, our boss told us that in the afternoon we would go to Mr Mason's farm in order to extract a horse's molar. Peggy had to stay in the surgery in order to work in the laboratory, checking blood and
25 urine.
In the late afternoon, we had to X-ray a cat and to hold a dog who got a tartar scaling. The last patient was a colourful bird who had caught a cold.

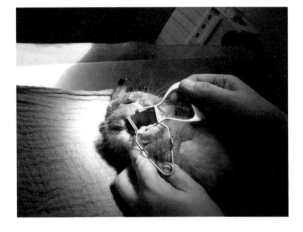

As you know, our job is not easy at all. We often
30 have to stand during work, and the animals do not always behave as you expect them to do. Besides, sometimes the pet owners can terrorize you more than the pet itself.
I remember one Monday morning, when Mrs Smith
35 brought Terry, a husky who suffered from diarrhoea and vomiting, and couldn't even stop this in our surgery. It was a challenging task for us to clean the mess, while Mrs Smith was having coffee with our boss in the kitchen.

40
You can certainly tell the class about your experiences as a vet's assistant. Are there any funny stories you can tell?

Please work in small groups. Make a list of ani-
45 mals being treated in your surgery. Give the English and German names and describe what is wrong with them and how they might be treated.

Comprehension – Please answer in complete sentences.

1. Who is Sissy and what happened to her in the surgery?
2. What did Peggy do during the operation?
3. What did Maureen do during the operation?
4. Describe how small animals are anaesthetized at Huntsville Animal Hospital.
5. What happened to Roger? What kind of animal is he?
6. What do turtles often get to survive the winter months?
7. Who was vaccinated against rabies?
8. What had to be done at Mr Mason's farm?
9. What did Peggy have to do in the afternoon?
10. What does a vet's assistant have to do when a cat has broken a leg?
11. Is the job as a vet's assistant easy? (Explain why/why not.)

Please translate the text into German.

Ein typischer Tag in unserer Praxis

Heute hatten wir 15 Tiere in unserer Praxis. …

Pair-work

Imagine these people and their pets have a seat in your waiting-room.

You happen to witness their conversation:

You wouldn't believe what has happened to my Bronco …

_____

_____

_____

_____

_____

_____

_____

Pair-work:

Try to sketch at least one typical part of your daily routine as a veterinarian's assistant by either

- drawing a cartoon or
- writing a poem or
- producing a wall-picture or
- …

and present your product to your classmates. They may ask questions – so be prepared to give some information about your creative work.

2.4 My job as a dental assistant

Good morning. Let me introduce our team to you: Dr Werner and his assistants Barbara and Nicole.

Before the first patient arrives, we have a look at the time schedule and plan our work. We have a list of patients who have an appointment with Dr Werner. Consulting hours are from 8.00 am to 5.00 pm.

When the first patient comes to the reception, Nicole crosses his name off the list, takes his file card out of the file card box, and puts the file card in consulting room 1.

Next please. As you know, almost everybody is a little bit nervous before the treatment begins. The patient needs your friendly smile and your helping hand.

The patient takes a seat in the dental chair and an assistant puts a white paper napkin around her neck. The basic instruments are on a tray: mirror, probe and a pair of tweezers.

We learn to choose the correct instruments for each treatment, but we don't put them all on the tray. An extraction forceps might shock patients. Therefore it is kept in the drawer behind the patient.

Please find the correct English expressions from the text above:

1. A person who is being treated by a doctor _____

2. An arrangement to see the
   dentist at a particular time _____

3. A plan that gives a list of appointments _____

4. The period of time in which
   a dentist sees patients _____

5. The place where appointments are given _____

6. A folded piece of paper in which
   documents like X-rays are kept _____

7. The place where patients are being treated _____

8. A piece of paper which is put
   around your neck in order
   to keep your clothes clean _____

9. A long thin metal instrument
   used to find cavities in teeth _____

10. Instruments are arranged on it _____

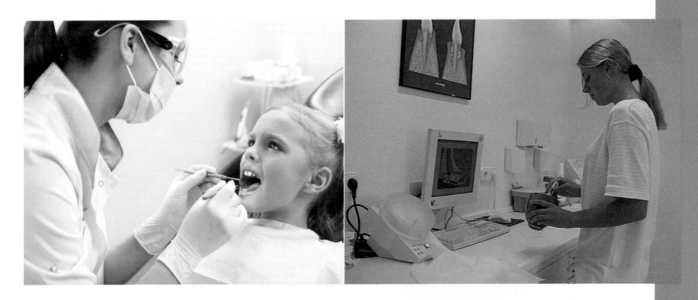

As a dental assistant you have to know how to mix filling materials, like amalgam and different cements.

We assist during the following kinds of treatment:

surgery	(extractions, osteotomies, implants, …)
periodontics	(the treatment of gum disease)
endodontics	(root canal treatment)
restorative dentistry	(filling cavities)
prosthetics	(making of dentures)
orthodontics	(moving and straightening teeth and correcting bite problems)

Please match the correct English and German expressions.

1. surgery
2. periodontics
3. endodontics
4. restorative dentistry
5. prosthetics
6. orthodontics

a Kieferorthopädie
b Konservierende Behandlung
c Prothetik
d Chirurgie
e Parodontalbehandlung
f Wurzelkanalbehandlung (Endodontie)

Sometimes we help the dentist by telling patients when and how to brush their teeth, how to use dental floss and a mouth rinse. The key to healthy teeth is prevention, not treatment. We show them pictures to make it easier for them to come to a decision concerning inlays, crowns or bridges.

Please translate:

ein Zahnarzt _____

Zähne putzen _____

Zahnseide _____

Munddusche _____

gesunde Zähne _____

Vorbeugung _____

Einlagefüllung _____

Krone _____

Brücke _____

What is the assistant's job?

Please describe what you see in the picture.

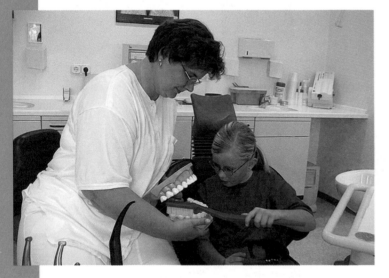

_____

_____

_____

_____

_____

_____

_____

_____

_____

_____

_____

_____

_____

1. What do you usually have for lunch? Please describe your typical midday meal and tell your classmates what you do during your midday break.
2. Please work in small groups. Make a list of healthy food which is good for your teeth. Make a list of unhealthy food which is bad for your teeth. Hang the lists on a wall in your classroom.

In the afternoon some of us are engaged in routine office work. We have a computer with three terminals. It is used to write invoices for the patients, to communicate with health insurances, and to cooperate with the KZV (Kassenzahnärztliche Vereinigung).

When you have passed your examination as a dental assistant, you are allowed to take X-rays of the patients' teeth.

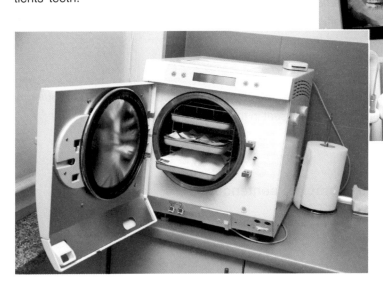

Disinfection, cleaning and sterilization of used instruments are tasks for the late afternoon. We need the instruments for the next day.

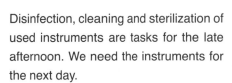

Please translate:

1. Rechnungen _____

2. Krankenversicherungen _____

3. Röntgenaufnahmen _____

4. Desinfektion _____

5. Reinigung _____

Pair-work

Try to sketch at least one typical part of your daily routine as a dental assistant by either

- drawing a cartoon or
- writing a poem or
- producing a wall-picture or
- …

and present your product to your classmates. They may ask questions – so be prepared to give some information about your creative work.

The American patient

It is 9.15. The telephone is ringing at Dr Berg's dental office. Ulrike is alone at the reception.

Ulrike: Guten Morgen. Praxis Dr Berg, Meier am Apparat.

Patient: This is Tom Craig. Do you speak English?

Ulrike: Yes, I do. How can I help you?

Patient: I have got problems with one of my teeth. I think I have to come for a treatment. I thought I could enjoy my holidays in Germany, sitting in beer gardens and having fun, but that was only a dream.

Ulrike: How long has your tooth been aching?

Patient: It has been aching for two days. I always hoped that it would stop, but unfortunately it didn't. All the whisky I drank did not help.

Ulrike: Whisky is certainly not the correct treatment. I suggest that you see the dentist. He will help you. Shall I arrange an appointment for you?

Patient: That would be great, although I am a little bit afraid of dentists and their instruments.

Ulrike: Let's see. What about 11.15?

Patient: Yes, that's perfect. Will you hold my hand?

Ulrike: I will do my best, but first of all let me write down your name. Could you spell it, please?

Patient: It's Craig, C - R - A - I - G. My first name is Tom. I come from New York.

Ulrike: Do you know how to find our dental office?

Patient: Yes, thank you. My hotel is just around the corner.

Ulrike: Fine. Is there anything else you would like to know?

Patient: Yes, how old are you?

Ulrike: I thought you would like to see my boss and not me. If you are a brave patient, I will tell you more about myself. But first, you will have to take a seat in the dental chair.

Patient: You are right. See you in a minute.

Ulrike: Good-bye.

Comprehension – Please answer in complete sentences.

1. Where does Tom Craig come from?
2. What did he actually want to do in Germany?
3. Why does he want to see a dentist?
4. What did he do to stop the toothache?
5. Was this the correct treatment?
6. Does Mr Craig like dentists?
7. Is he interested in Ulrike? Please explain your answer.

Dentists in Toronto

Please fill in the missing words.

If you need crowns or bridges you can go to Dr _____ or to _____.

Dr Carcao is a specialist in _____ for adults and _____.

Laser assisted dentistry is offered by Dr _____. He also treats _____ disease.

If you want to have an evening appointment you can phone Dr _____ and _____.

If you prefer to see a dentist on Saturdays you can make an appointment with Dr _____,

Dr _____ and _____.

Dr Kostiuk's phone number is _____.

He welcomes _____.

Dr _____ offers bleaching, _____ veneers and hypnosis.

Call number _____.

Invisible _____ are available at Dr Carcao's surgery, which is located in _____,

west of Ossington _____.

At Thorncliffe Dental Centre you can pay by _____ card.

PEKAR THOMAS DR

LASER
ASSISTED
DENTISTRY

MINIMIZES DRILLING &
ANESTHESIA
EARLY TREATMENT OF
PERIODONTAL DISEASE

290 Glendale ------------ StCatharines (416) 687-9454
If Busy Call ---------------------- Thorold 416 277-7377

SBWY.

Bloor St. W	●
Charles St.	
Irwin Ave.	(P)
Wellesley St. W	●

Yonge St.

N ↑ SBWY.

Please translate the text into German.
You may use a dictionary.

Wenn Sie Kronen oder Brücken brauchen,

_____

_____

_____

_____

_____

2.5 A day in the pharmacy

Melanie and Daniela have been working in Mr Sorg's pharmacy in Goslar for four months. They are his trainees.

Melanie: Good morning, Daniela. Did you enjoy the party yesterday?

Daniela: *Good morning, Melanie. Yes, the party was actually wonderful, but I am still a little bit tired. I went to bed at 2 a.m.*

Melanie: Oh, you won't have time to sleep at work today. Our boss has a huge list of things we will have to manage on this beautiful winter day.

Mr Sorg: *Good morning, you two. Today you will have to work rather fast in order to manage everything. First of all, I want you to run errands. Melanie, please go to the bank and to the copy shop. Daniela, you have to go to the post office and to Mrs Drechsler's surgery. She needs hydrogen peroxide and gauze bandages.*

Melanie: Mr Sorg, when shall we check the invoices?

Mr Sorg: *After you return you will have to do office work. I know that you like to work with the computer. You will check the invoices and also unwrap the delivery from our wholesaler, sort the drugs and put them into the correct shelves and drawers. Maybe there will be items we will have to send back to our wholesaler. You should order aspirin and other drugs we need by phone.*

Daniela: *What shall I do while Melanie does this work?*

Mr Sorg: *Please control the best-before dates of our remedies and teas. Afterwards, please clean the shelves and help me to produce ointments. You will have lunch between 1 p.m. and 2 p.m.*

Daniela and Melanie are enjoying their midday break at the Christmas fair. After arriving at the pharmacy, they ask Mr Sorg for their tasks in the afternoon.

Mr Sorg: *In the afternoon, you two can work together. First you have to weigh the following teas and tea-mixtures: stinging nettle, yarrow, thyme, sage, horsetail, fennel, camomile, peppermint, coltsfoot, and cough tea.*
Secondly, stock up on linseed, suppositories, ointments, cough syrup, cough drops, and cough sweets. At the moment, there is a heavy demand for cough medicine. As you know, almost everybody seems to suffer from the flu this winter.

Daniela: *What about our window display?*

Mr Sorg: *Good that you mention it. If you have time in the late afternoon, you will help me decorate the window with posters and information about the respiratory system, its diseases, like bronchitis, and remedies for these diseases.*

Melanie: Mr Sorg, did you forget that we have to stamp and display the customer magazines for January?

Mr Sorg: *No, I didn't, but you won't have enough time to do this today. You can stamp the magazines tomorrow, together with the hundreds of prescriptions we will have to stamp as well.*

At 6.30 p.m. Daniela and Melanie leave their workplace. They will be spending the next few hours together, watching a movie and eating at an Italian restaurant. They are not only colleagues, but good friends, who enjoy working and having fun together.

Here is a list of German expressions. Please find the matching English expressions from the text above. You may use a dictionary.

1. Apotheke _____

2. Auszubildende _____

3. Botengänge, kleine Besorgungen machen

_____

4. Arztpraxis _____

5. Wasserstoffsuperoxid _____

6. Mullbinden _____

7. Rechnungen prüfen _____

8. Büroarbeit _____

9. eine Warensendung auspacken

_____

10. Großhändler _____

11. Medikamente einsortieren _____

_____

12. Regale _____

13. Schubladen _____

14. Artikel _____

15. Aspirin telefonisch bestellen

_____

16. Verfallsdaten kontrollieren

_____

17. Heilmittel _____

18. Regale säubern _____

19. Salben herstellen _____

20. Aufgaben _____

21. Tee und Teemischungen abwiegen

_____

22. Brennessel _____

23. Schafgarbe _____

24. Thymian _____

25. Salbei _____

26. Schachtelhalm _____

27. Fenchel _____

28. Kamille _____

29. Pfefferminze _____

30. Huflattich _____

31. Hustentee _____

32. Hustensirup _____

33. Hustentropfen _____

34. Hustenbonbons _____

35. Leinsamenvorrat auffüllen

_____

36. große Nachfrage nach

_____

37. Zäpfchen _____

38. unter Grippe leiden _____

39. Schaufensterauslage _____

40. Atmungssystem _____

41. Krankheiten _____

42. Kundenzeitschriften stempeln

_____

43. auslegen _____

44. Rezepte _____

45. Arbeitsplatz _____

46. Kollegen _____

Please decide whether the following sentences are true or false.

1. Melanie and Daniela are working at Mr Sorg's surgery.   _____*false*_____

2. Daniela enjoyed the party.   _____

3. Daniela has got enough time to sleep at work.   _____

4. The first task for Melanie is to check the invoices.   _____

5. Melanie hates to work with the computer.   _____

6. Melanie will put the drugs into the correct shelves and drawers.   _____

7. There is no demand for cough medicine at the moment.   _____

8. Melanie has got enough time to stamp and to display the customer magazines.   _____

If the sentence is false, please write the correct sentence in your exercise book.

Comprehension – Please answer in complete sentences.

1. What does Daniela do while Melanie does the office work?
2. When is lunch for Daniela and Melanie?
3. Where are Daniela and Melanie having lunch?
4. When and where do you usually have lunch?
5. Describe the window display of Mr Sorg's pharmacy.
6. You are being trained at a certain pharmacy. Describe one of your window displays you liked most.
7. What does Melanie want to do with the customer magazines?
8. What are the contents of these magazines? Why do customers like to read them?
9. What will Daniela and Melanie do after work?
10. Do you spend your free time with colleagues? What do you like to do with them?
11. Describe your tasks at the pharmacy.

Pair-work

Try to sketch at least one typical part of your daily routine as a PKA by either

    drawing a cartoon or

    writing a poem or

    producing a wall-picture or

    …

and present your product to your classmates. They may ask questions – so be prepared to give some information about your creative work.

The pharmacy

Yesterday …

… and today.

1. Please have a look at the pictures and describe both of them.

2. In which ways does today's pharmacy differ from yesterday's pharmacy?

3. Please describe the pharmacy where you work. You may draw a picture.

4. What do you know about the system of selling drugs in Canada and in the United States of America?

5. How has the internet changed the selling of drugs worldwide? Give examples.

2.6 My job as a geriatric nurse

Nobody really thinks that working in an old people's home is an easy job. When you ask young people in the street, whether they want to work with old people, they hesitate. Who wants to see people dying, witness pain, misery and loneliness? Almost everybody shivers when imagining the smell of old people's homes and most people are afraid of confused residents.

Only those persons can work successfully in an old people's home who don't take problems home, who are emotionally strong and who have a lot of patience and physical strength.

I am one of these geriatric nurses. It is my dream job and my name is Alexandra. We have 37 residents in our home Rose Garden. Most of them are in their eighties or nineties. I have to get up very early in the morning. When I have the morning shift, I start at 7 a.m. I help the residents to get up and assist them with washing. I help them getting dressed and serve them breakfast.

In the morning I read the newspaper to some residents. Sadly, there is not enough time for talks although most residents like to talk, especially about their past and their families. Mrs Gowan, for example, has nobody who visits her. Her husband died years ago and her children and grandchildren live 250 kilometres away. She wants to tell me about her past, but I have to do the documentation, order medicine from the pharmacy, collect dirty towels, sheets and bedclothes, take out garbage or do wound management. We don't have enough employees. Sometimes I am even too exhausted to have a conversation. My break is from ten to ten-fifteen.

Before lunch, the residents get drinks they like to have. I assist them by going to the dining-room. After lunch, residents can have a nap. In the afternoon, there is coffee or tea. Every other day we have occupational therapy. Twice a week our physiotherapist Berit offers some gymnastics for the fitter ones. Sometimes we even have trips to shops or to the cinema. Supper is from five-thirty to six o'clock.

Some residents may have a bath or a shower. I help them undress and prepare them for bed, assist them by taking out their prostheses and hearing aids.

Please find the correct English expressions from the text above:

1. eine Altenpflegerin/ein Altenpfleger _____

2. ein Altersheim _____

3. Schmerz _____

4. Elend _____

5. Einsamkeit _____

6. Geruch _____

7. verwirrte Bewohner _____

8. Geduld _____

9. körperliche Kraft _____

10. Frühdienst _____

11. Bettlaken _____

12. Bettzeug _____

13. Wundversorgung _____

14. Beschäftigungstherapie _____

15. Zahnprothese _____

16. Hörgerät _____

Comprehension – Please answer in complete sentences.

1. Why do young people hesitate to work in an old people's home?

2. What kind of qualifications must a person have to work successfully in an old people's home?

3. Did Alexandra want to have the job as a geriatric nurse?

4. What is the name of the home she works at?

5. How many residents live there?

6. How old are the residents Alexandra cares for?

7. When does the morning shift start?

8. Make a list of all the tasks Alexandra has to do in the morning.

9. Do you offer occupational therapy in your home? Describe what kind of things old people can do to occupy themselves.

10. How does your work routine differ from Alexandra's work routine?

Please describe what you see in the pictures.

A)

B)

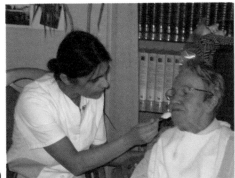

C)

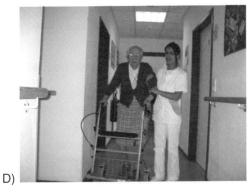

D)

E)

F)

G)

H)

I)

Pair-work

Try to sketch a typical part of your daily routine as a geriatric nurse by either

- drawing a cartoon
- writing a poem
- writing a story
- producing a wall-paper.

To get more information about the job of an old people's nurse in English speaking countries use a search engine such as google.com.

Create a brochure of the old people's home you work at. Illustrate your texts with pictures.

Biography work: Work in groups and devise a questionnaire with 10 questions you want to ask a resident about his/her life. Choose a resident at your workplace and interview him/her. Find out how his/her life has changed since his/her retirement. Make notes during the interview, translate them into English and make a role play. One of you is the resident, the other one is the old people's nurse.

Discuss the following statements about positive and negative aspects of getting old:

Positive
- You don't have to work anymore.
- You don't have to get up early in the morning.
- You have much time for your hobbies, friends and family.
- You have time to travel.

Negative
- You need help and support.
- You forget things and become confused.
- You lose physical strength and get ill.
- You are lonely because nobody wants to talk to old people.
- Society does not value old people.
- Your friends die.

Working in a home care team

Claudia:	Good morning, Frau Burgdorf. Did you sleep well last night?
Frau Burgdorf:	*Thank you very much. I watched television until two o'clock at night.*
Claudia:	What was on?
Frau Burgdorf:	*There was a film about England. You know that I had a boyfriend from England during World War II. He wanted to marry me but my father did not want to let me go. So I stayed at the farm and never married. Now I am ninety-two.*
Claudia:	So you had time to think about your past. How nice.
Frau Burgdorf:	*I think so. If I had not had this pain in my chest. I coughed the whole night.*
Claudia:	I am going to rub a special ointment into your skin. It will help you to breathe through. You still have got your cold. Maybe you should drink a cup of peppermint tea with honey.
Frau Burgdorf:	*Yes, I would really like to have a cup of tea after being washed.*
Claudia:	Please hand me your blanket and your bed jacket. I am going to wash you now.
Frau Burgdorf:	*Here you are. Could you please take the coconut shower lotion and the soft body cream?*
Claudia:	Where can I find these things?
Frau Burgdorf:	*They are in the bathroom.*
Claudia:	Fine.
Frau Burgdorf:	*Oh, this is nice. Thank you very much.*
Claudia:	When do you want your hair to be washed?
Frau Burgdorf:	*Friday would be good. My nephew and his wife are going to visit me at the weekend.*
Claudia:	Yes, this is fine. So, I am now going to brush your hair. Have you got a comb in one of these drawers?
Frau Burgdorf:	*Oh yes, in the upper drawer of my bedside table are my combs, my paper tissues, my spectacles and my nail scissors.*
Claudia:	Do you want your finger-nails to be cut today?

Frau Burgdorf:	*No, thank you. But I really would like to use lipstick and perfume today.*
Claudia:	May I help you with the lipstick?
Frau Burgdorf:	*That would be nice. But first I want to dress.*
Claudia:	What do you want to wear?
Frau Burgdorf:	*I really would like to wear my grey skirt and perhaps the yellow blouse.*
Claudia:	I think the yellow blouse suits you, but I'm afraid it could be too cold. The blouse has got short sleeves. 
Frau Burgdorf:	*You are right. I should rather wear a long sleeved jumper today.*
Claudia:	What colour do you prefer?
Frau Burgdorf:	*I prefer blue. The one I like is in the wardrobe. It is pure wool.*
Claudia:	Is it this one here?
Frau Burgdorf:	*Yes, it is. Please hand me the pink scarf and my blue shoes.*
Claudia:	Here you are.
Frau Burgdorf:	*Thank you very much.*
Claudia:	Let me help you with the zipper of your skirt.
Frau Burgdorf:	*Oh, the skirt doesn`t fit me any more. It is too small.*
Claudia:	What a pity!
Frau Burgdorf:	*I should stop eating sweets and drinking my Madeira wine.*
Claudia:	I don't think so. Just try another skirt. How do you like this cream one?
Frau Burgdorf:	*Oh yes, it fits perfectly to the jumper. Claudia, could you please give me my tights and my golden brooch from the drawer?*
Claudia:	Yes, of course. What a wonderful brooch!
Frau Burgdorf:	*It is a gift from my mother. I have had it for about forty years.*
Claudia:	So, what will you get for lunch today?
Frau Burgdorf:	*Well, today they serve fish, mashed potatoes, peas, carrots and cauliflower. I can swallow this meal easily. And I like it. For dessert there is fruit salad. Without meals on wheels I could not live my life so independently.*
Claudia:	That is right.
Frau Burgdorf:	*In the afternoon Frau Gutsche will visit me. She promised to bring her famous cheese cake.*
Claudia:	So this will be a nice day for you, won't it. I hope you enjoy it. Have a nice time.
Frau Burgdorf:	*You too. And thank you very much.*

Translate the dialogue into German.

Please discuss the following statements in class:

- There is nothing better for old people than television.
- An old people's home can never be like a real home.
- In the future we will have an increase in home care teams, because people want to stay at home as long as possible.
- You can understand your past when you understand your grandparents.
- Touch old people and they will feel better. It feels like magic.
- I would rather die than live in an old people`s home for fifteen years.
- Only rich people can afford a qualified home.

2.7 Internet Research

In Unit 2 you got to know special vocabulary you will need in order to describe your daily routine as a doctor's assistant, a dental assistant, a veterinarian's assistant, an assistant at a pharmacy or a geriatric nurse. There is a large number of these assistants in the United States and in the United Kingdom. You can get detailed information by using the internet. Use **www.google.com**

Pair-work

Find the address of the American Dental Assistants' Association and ask for information on being a Dental Assistant in the USA by using e-mail.

Find the address of the American Association of Medical Assistants and ask for information by using e-mail.

Find the address of the British Veterinary Nursing Association and ask for information by using e-mail. Search the internet for information on geriatric nursing.

Grammar Revision

Irregular Verbs

There are a lot of irregular verbs. Here are some which can be useful for your work in the surgery or in the pharmacy.

Please fill in the missing forms.

	Present Tense	Past Tense	Past Participle
sein	to be	_____	been
werden	to become	became	_____
beginnen	to _____	began	begun
bluten	to _____	bled	bled
brechen	to break	_____	_____
bringen	to bring	_____	_____
brennen	to burn	burnt	_____
_____	to buy	_____	_____
fangen	to _____	caught	caught
auswählen	to _____	chose	chosen
kommen	to come	_____	come
_____	to cost	cost	cost
tun	to _____	_____	_____
trinken	to drink	_____	_____
essen	to eat	_____	_____
fallen	to fall	fell	_____
fühlen	to _____	felt	felt
finden	to _____	_____	_____
verbieten	to _____	forbade	forbidden
vergessen	to _____	_____	_____
bekommen	to get	_____	_____
geben	to _____	_____	_____
gehen	to _____	_____	_____
haben	to have	_____	_____
_____	to hear	heard	heard
halten	to hold	_____	_____
verletzen	to _____	_____	_____

_____	to kneel	knelt	knelt
wissen	to _____	_____	_____
liegen	to _____	lay	lain
machen	to make	_____	_____
bezahlen	to _____	paid	_____
setzen, legen, stellen	to _____	_____	_____
lesen	to _____	_____	_____
_____	to ring	rang	rung
sagen	to _____	said	said
sehen	to see	_____	_____
verkaufen	to _____	sold	sold
schicken	to _____	sent	sent
zeigen	to _____	showed	shown
schließen	to _____	shut	shut
sitzen	to sit	_____	_____
_____	to sleep	slept	slept
riechen	to _____	smelt	smelt
sprechen	to speak	_____	_____
buchstabieren	to spell	_____	_____
stehen	to _____	stood	stood
nehmen	to take	_____	_____
erzählen	to _____	told	told
_____	to think	_____	_____
verstehen	to _____	understood	_____
weinen	to _____	wept	wept
schreiben	to _____	_____	_____

Grammar Revision

The Active Tenses

Please translate:

Present Tense (Präsens, Gegenwart)	1. Ich arbeite.	*I work.*
	2. Er arbeitet.	
	3. Sie arbeiten nicht.	
	4. Arbeiten sie?	
	5. Arbeitet er?	
Past Tense (Vergangenheit)	1. Ich arbeitete.	
	2. Er arbeitete.	
	3. Er arbeitete nicht.	
	4. Arbeitete sie?	
Present Perfect (vollendete Gegenwart)	1. Wir haben gearbeitet.	
	2. Er hat gearbeitet.	
	3. Hat sie gearbeitet?	
Past Perfect (vollendete Vergangenheit)	1. Ich hatte gearbeitet.	
	2. Hatte er gearbeitet?	
Future I (Zukunft)	1. Ich werde arbeiten.	
	2. Sie wird nicht arbeiten.	
	3. Wird er arbeiten?	
Future II (vollendete Zukunft)	1. Ich werde gearbeitet haben.	
	2. Wird sie gearbeitet haben?	
Conditional I (Konditional I)	1. Ich würde arbeiten.	
	2. Würde er arbeiten?	
	3. Sie würde nicht arbeiten.	
Conditional II (Konditional II)	1. Ich würde gearbeitet haben.	
	2. Er würde gearbeitet haben.	
	3. Würde sie gearbeitet haben?	

Grammar Revision

Please write the sentence in the different tenses.

She / to be / at the vocational school.

1. Present Tense   *She is at the vocational school.* _____

2. Present Perfect _____

3. Past Tense   _____

4. Past Perfect   _____

5. Future I   _____

6. Future II   _____

7. Conditional I   _____

8. Conditional II   _____

Please put the verb into the correct form.

1. to make	3. Pers. Singular	Future II	*he/she will have made*
2. to know	1. Pers. Plural	Past Tense	
3. to bring	2. Pers. Singular	Present Perfect	
4. to say	3. Pers. Singular	Conditional II	
5. to show	2. Pers. Plural	Future I	
6. to forget	3. Pers. Singular	Past Perfect	
7. to bleed	1. Pers. Singular	Conditional I	
8. to eat	3. Pers. Singular	Past Tense	
9. to hear	1. Pers. Singular	Past Perfect	
10. to understand	3. Pers. Singular	Future II	

Please translate:

1. Wird sie die Praxis verkaufen? _____

2. Morgen wird er sein Auto verkauft haben. _____

3. Die Patientin kauft immer teure Medikamente. _____

4. Wie oft gehst Du ins Kino? _____

5. Magst Du den Patienten? _____

6. Er nahm seine Tabletten nicht. _____

7. Weinte der Patient? _____

What do you know about your body and its functions?

3.1 The body's systems

Did you ever wonder what you are made of? About what is inside of you? Your body is a very complicated machine. In order to understand how it works, you have to know some fundamental facts about it.

Cells make up the tissues of your body.

Tissues make up organs. Every organ has a special job.

5 Organs make up organ systems.

The **nervous system**, especially the brain, controls our actions, thoughts and feelings and tells the body what to do. Without our brain we would feel neither love nor anger, and life would be totally boring.

Each side of the brain controls the opposite side of the body. The nervous system gets messages and sends out messages as small electrical impulses. Your body works by getting instructions from the brain.

10 Nerves tell the muscles what to do. On the one hand, your brain can tell your arm to move and to stroke a patient or your boyfriend. This is a conscious decision. You don't have to do it, but you want to do it. The muscles will move your arm.

On the other hand, you cannot tell your lungs to breathe or your stomach to digest the cheeseburger you have just eaten. Digestion, breathing, heart beating and blood circulation are autonomous functions.

15 The **digestive system** is composed of the mouth, the throat, the stomach and the intestines. It also includes the liver, the gall bladder and the pancreas. The liver is the largest gland of the body. It produces bile.

The **urinary system** cleans blood and urine. It consists of the kidneys, the bladder, the ureter and the urethra. The kidneys work like filters and remove wastes from the body.

The **respiratory system** consists of the nose, the windpipe and the lungs. The blood transports oxygen
20 into the lungs.

The **circulation system** includes the heart, the blood vessels (arteries, veins) and the lymph vessels.

The heart pumps the blood through the body. Blood takes oxygen and nutrients to the cells and takes waste products from them. Arteries carry the blood from the heart to the cells, veins carry the blood back to the heart. The blood is purified by the liver and the kidneys.

25 The **endocrine system** produces hormones that tell the organs to fulfil certain tasks. Glands like the pancreas release hormones. Hormones like estrogen, insulin, adrenaline and cortisone swim in your blood to the organs.

The **male reproductive system** includes the penis and the testes.

The **female reproductive system** includes the uterus, the ovaries, the fallopian tubes and the vagina.

30 The **immune system** defends the body against attacks from microorganisms (bacteria, viruses and fungi).

The **skeleton** protects the organs. It consists of 206 bones, joints and cartilage. It works together with the muscles and the skin.

The **skin** is the largest organ of the body.

Please translate the text.
Die Systeme des Körpers
Haben Sie sich jemals gefragt, woraus Sie bestehen? ...

Parts of the body and their functions

Adrenalin	adrenaline	**Harnapparat**	urinary system
Arm	arm	**Harnleiter**	ureter
Arterie	artery	**Harnröhre**	urethra
atmen	to breathe	**Haut**	skin
Atmung	respiration, breathing	**Herz**	heart
Atmungssystem	respiratory system	**Hoden**	testis, plural: testes
Auge	eye	**Hormon**	hormone
Augenlid	eyelid	**Hormonsystem**	endocrine system
Backenzahn	molar	**Hüfte**	hip
Bakterien	bacteria	**Immunsystem**	immune system
Bandscheibe	intervertebral disc	**Insulin**	insulin
Bauchspeicheldrüse	pancreas	**Kehle**	throat
Becken	pelvis	**Kehlkopf**	larynx
Bein	leg	**Kiefer**	jaw
Blase	bladder	**Kieferhöhle**	maxillary sinus
Blinddarm	appendix	**Kinn**	chin
Blut	blood	**Kleinstlebewesen**	microorganism
Blutdruck	blood pressure	**Knie**	knee
Blutgefäße	blood vessels	**Knöchel**	ankle
Brust	breast, chest	**Knochen**	bone
Brustbein	breastbone	**Knorpel**	cartilage
Brustkorb	thorax	**Kopf**	head
Cortison	cortisone	**Körper**	body
Darm	intestine	**Kreislauf**	circulation
Dünndarm	small intestine	**Kreislaufsystem**	circulation system
Dickdarm	large intestine	**Kreuzbein**	sacrum
Daumen	thumb	**Leber**	liver
Drüse	gland	**Lippe**	lip
Eckzahn	canine	**Luftröhre**	windpipe
Eierstock	ovary	**Lunge**	lung
Eileiter	fallopian tube	**Lymphgefäße**	lymph vessels
Ellenbogen	elbow	**Magen**	stomach
Ferse	heel	**Mandeln**	tonsils
Finger	finger	**Mastdarm**	rectum
Fuß	foot, plural: feet	**Milz**	spleen
Gallenblase	gall bladder	**Mund**	mouth
Gallensaft	bile	**Muskel**	muscle
Gaumen	palate	**Nährstoff**	nutrient
Gebärmutter	uterus	**Nagel**	nail
Gehirn	brain	**Nase**	nose
Gelenk	joint	**Nerven**	nerves
Genick, Nacken	neck	**Nervensystem**	nervous system
Geschlechtsorgane	sex organs, reproductive system	**Niere**	kidney
Gesicht	face	**Oberkiefer**	upper jaw
Gewebe	tissue	**Oberschenkel**	thigh
Haare	hair	**Östrogen**	estrogen
Hand	hand	**Ohr**	ear
Handgelenk	wrist	**Organ**	organ
		Penis	penis

Pilze	fungi	**Unterleib**	abdomen
Prämolar	premolar	**Urin**	urine
reinigen	to purify	**Vene**	vein
Rippe	rib	**verdauen**	to digest
Rücken	back	**Verdauung**	digestion
Rückenmark	spinal cord	**Verdauungssystem**	digestive system
Sauerstoff	oxygen	**Viren**	viruses
Schädel	skull	**Wade**	calf
Scheide	vagina	**Wange**	cheek
Schienbein	tibia	**Weisheitszahn**	wisdom tooth
Schlackenstoffe	waste products	**Wirbelsäule**	spine
Schlüsselbein	collar bone, clavicle	**Wurzelhaut**	periodontal membrane
Schneidezahn	incisor	**Wurzelzement**	cement
Schulter	shoulder	**Zahn**	tooth, plural: teeth
Schulterblatt	shoulder-blade	**Zahnbein**	dentine
Schwangerschaft	pregnancy	**Zahnfleisch**	gum
Sehne	tendon, sinew	**Zahnhals**	neck
Skelett	skeleton	**Zahnkrone**	crown
Speiseröhre	gullet	**Zahnmark**	pulp
Stirn	forehead	**Zahnschmelz**	enamel
Stirnhöhle	frontal cavity	**Zahnwurzel**	root
Stoffwechsel	metabolism	**Zehe**	toe
Stuhlgang	bowel movement	**Zelle**	cell
Trommelfell	ear-drum	**Zunge**	tongue
Unterkiefer	lower jaw	**Zwölffingerdarm**	duodenum

What are these parts of the body called?

Please fill in the correct expressions.

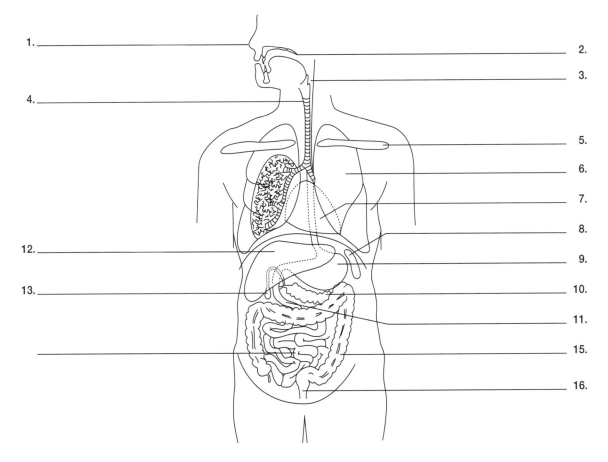

1. _____
2. _____
3. _____
4. _____
5. _____
6. _____
7. _____
8. _____
9. _____
10. _____
11. _____
12. _____
13. _____
15. _____
16. _____

Please complete the following sentences with the correct expressions.

1. A part of the respiratory system is
   - ☐ the heart
   - ☐ the stomach
   - ☐ the windpipe
   - ☐ the brain

2. The system which defends the body against attacks from microorganisms is
   - ☐ the urinary system
   - ☐ the skeleton
   - ☐ the immune system
   - ☐ the digestive system

3. The organ which beats faster when you are in love is
   - ☐ the lung
   - ☐ the heart
   - ☐ the nose
   - ☐ the stomach

4. The largest gland of the body is
   - ☐ the gall bladder
   - ☐ the pancreas
   - ☐ the liver
   - ☐ the testis

5. The largest organ of the body is
   - ☐ the skeleton
   - ☐ the skin
   - ☐ the lung
   - ☐ the brain

6. Elbows and knees are
   - ☐ blood vessels
   - ☐ bones
   - ☐ joints
   - ☐ cartilage

7. The blood vessels which carry the blood from the heart to the cells are called
   - ☐ blood pressures
   - ☐ arteries
   - ☐ veins
   - ☐ circulatory systems

8. The gland which produces insulin is called
   - ☐ the testis
   - ☐ the ovary
   - ☐ the pancreas
   - ☐ the liver

Scrambled Words

Please write down the correct words and translate them.

1. ISKN _____skin_____ _____Haut_____
2. MRA _____ _____
3. IEDYNK _____ _____
4. REA _____ _____
5. VELIR _____ _____
6. SOLREDUH _____ _____
7. CLUMSE _____ _____

8. BADERDL _____ _____
9. NITOJ _____ _____
10. TEUGNO _____ _____
11. WOBLE _____ _____
12. EKSLOTEN _____ _____
13. PIEPNIWD _____ _____

3.2 The skeleton

What are these parts of the skeleton called?

Please fill in the correct expressions.

1. _____

2. _____

3. _____

4. _____

5. _____

6. _____

7. _____

8. _____

9. _____

10. _____

11. _____

12. _____

3.3 The teeth

Hello!

I am a tooth. As you know, I am made up of a crown and a root. My crown is above the gum, my root is inside the jawbone. Between the root and the crown is my neck.

There are a lot of bacteria in your mouth. If you eat toffees and don't brush your teeth, sugar and bacteria will produce acids that cause a hole in my enamel. Oh, by the way, enamel covers the outside of my crown.

5 Although it is the hardest substance produced in the body, acids can destroy the enamel and a cavity results. Under my enamel is the dentine, a bone-like substance.

In my centre there is a material called pulp. It contains blood and lymph vessels and nerve endings.

My root is covered with cement.

I am a molar. The other guys beside me are pre-molars, canines, and incisors. Next to me is my best friend,
10 the wisdom tooth. There are eight of us in each half of the jaw.

Please fill in the correct expressions.

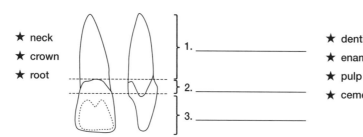

★ neck
★ crown
★ root

1. _____
2. _____
3. _____

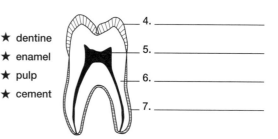

★ dentine
★ enamel
★ pulp
★ cement

4. _____
5. _____
6. _____
7. _____

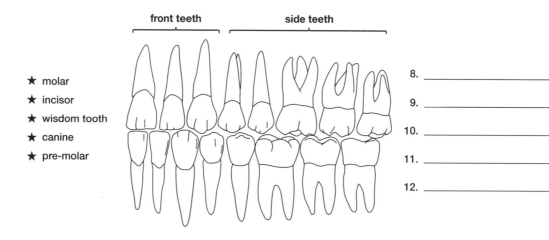

front teeth   side teeth

★ molar
★ incisor
★ wisdom tooth
★ canine
★ pre-molar

8. _____
9. _____
10. _____
11. _____
12. _____

Please complete the following sentences with the correct expressions.

1. The part of the tooth which is inside the jawbone is called
   ☐ neck
   ☐ root
   ☐ crown

2. A molar is
   ☐ a side tooth
   ☐ a front tooth
   ☐ a jawbone

3. The hardest substance in the body is
   ☐ bone
   ☐ dentine
   ☐ enamel

4. The centre of a tooth is called
   ☐ dentine
   ☐ cement
   ☐ pulp

5. A molar in the upper jaw has
   ☐ one root
   ☐ two roots
   ☐ three roots

6. Enamel can be destroyed by
   ☐ acids
   ☐ bacteria
   ☐ sugar

Scrambled Words

Please write down the correct words and translate them.

1. NMTEEC   *cement*   *Wurzelzement*

2. NITDENE _____ _____

3. MANELE _____ _____

4. WRONC _____ _____

5. NCAIEN _____ _____

6. KCNE _____ _____

7. PLUP _____ _____

8. OTOR _____ _____

9. AWJ _____ _____

10. RALMO _____ _____

11. ROSICNI _____ _____

12. THOTO _____ _____

13. MUG _____ _____

3.4 Internet Research

Make an Internet Research in order to get more information about the human body.

Use **www.bbc.co.uk/science/humanbody**

Here you find interesting details about the human body and the mind. You can build a skeleton, stretch some muscles and organise the organs in an interactive body. You can also discover how the body changes during puberty.
Try the skeleton-, organs- and muscle game, try some psychological tests and explore your memory.

In the skeleton game you have to get the joints and bones in the right places. In the organs game you can plumb together your organs in a 3D jigsaw puzzle. In the muscle game you put the muscles into the right places.
Every game takes about 5 to 10 minutes.

Use **www.visiblebody.com**

Here you find a complete fully interactive 3D human anatomy model.
You can take the tour or try the demo.
Use **www.youtube.com** to find videos on the digestive system

Use **www.google.com** to find a medical dictionary and fill in the blanks with the correct words. Select a word from the list in parentheses after each blank.

The _____ (sponge, spine, sperm, spat) is the most important bone in the body.
The bones that make up the spine are the _____ (volleys, ribs, vertebrae, collar bones).
On top of the spine is the _____ (jawbone, skull, forehead, elbow).
The top bones of the spine build the (nerves, muscles, neck, ankle).
The _____ (rib, root, rough, round) bones are connected with the vertebrae below the neck.
_____(Five, Seven, Two, Seventeen) vertebrae support the lower back.

Use **www.simplyteeth.com**

Here you find an A–Z index. Click on the links about teeth and gums.
You find pictures and a dental dictionary.

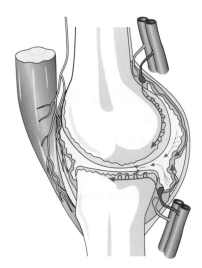

How can you help and support?

4.1 Giving appointments on the phone

Pair-work

Imagine you were in London and suddenly got a pain in your chest. You would have to call a doctor.

What would you expect from a doctor's assistant on the phone?

Write down four aspects on four cards; each of you should present two aspects to the class.

Before answering the phone, you shouldn't forget that you don't have the help of your body language to get your message across.

So have a smile on your face when you are on the phone. – Your voice will sound a lot friendlier.

**The phone is ringing.
You pick it up.**

Give surgery name and your name:

_____

_____

Patient:	*Hello. This is Mable Baker.*
Doctor's assistant / Dental assistant:	Hello. What can I do for you?
Patient:	*I'm calling to make an appointment with Dr* _____
Doctor's assistant / Dental assistant:	Yes, sure. When would you like to come?
Patient:	*What about Monday?*
Doctor's assistant / Dental assistant:	I'm sorry, but there are no appointments free on Monday.
Patient:	*Oh, what a pity.*
Doctor's assistant / Dental assistant:	What about Tuesday?
Patient:	*Tuesday will be fine. May I come at nine o'clock?*
Doctor's assistant / Dental assistant:	Yes, that's fine, Mrs Baker.
Patient:	*Okay, then. See you on Tuesday. And thank you very much.*
Doctor's assistant / Dental assistant:	You are welcome. Thanks for calling.
Patient:	*Bye-bye.*

4.2 Telephone phrases

Please translate the English expressions into German and learn them by heart.

Hello, I'd like to speak to ..., please.
Hello, could I speak to ..., please? _____
Hello, could I talk to ..., please?

Hello, could you put me
through to ..., please? _____

The reason I'm calling is ... _____

Who's calling, please? _____

Could I have your name, please? _____

One moment, please.
Just a second. _____

Hold the line, please. _____

I'll try to connect you. _____

I'll put you through. _____

I'm afraid that isn't possible. _____

Can I take your number? _____

Can we call you back later? _____

I'm sorry, I didn't catch that. _____

Sorry, could you
repeat that, please? _____

Could you speak a bit
more slowly, please? _____

Could you speak
up a bit, please? _____

I'm sorry, the line is busy.
I'm sorry, the line is engaged. _____

Can I take a message? _____

Would you like
to leave a message? _____

4.3 The "little helpers" when telephoning

When you spell a name in Germany on the phone, you often say *A wie Anton, B wie Berta, C wie Cäsar, D wie Dora, …*

In English you should say:

A for Alfa	**H** for Hotel	**O** for Oscar	**V** for Victor
B for Bravo	**I** for India	**P** for Papa	**W** for Whiskey
C for Charlie	**J** for Juliett	**Q** for Quebec	**X** for X-ray
D for Delta	**K** for Kilo	**R** for Romeo	**Y** for Yankee
E for Echo	**L** for Lima	**S** for Sierra	**Z** for Zulu
F for Foxtrot	**M** for Mike	**T** for Tango	
G for Golf	**N** for November	**U** for Uniform	

Spelling Practice

1. Spell your first name and your family name.
2. Spell the name of one of your classmates.
3. Spell the name of your boss and let your classmates write down his or her name on a piece of paper.
4. Spell the name of the city and the street where your surgery/pharmacy is situated.
5. Spell the names of the following patients: Miller, Robinson, Holmes, Lewis, Smith, Jones, Stewart.

Number Practice

Please write the following numbers in words.

1 = *one*	7 = _____	13 = _____	19 = _____
2 = _____	8 = _____	14 = _____	20 = _____
3 = _____	9 = _____	15 = _____	25 = _____
4 = _____	10 = _____	16 = _____	30 = _____
5 = _____	11 = _____	17 = _____	40 = _____
6 = _____	12 = _____	18 = _____	50 = _____

Dates

You can say   June 6 (th) = June the sixth
                     6 (th) June = the sixth of June

Ordinal number – Please write them in words.

1st = *the first*	6th = _____
2nd = _____	7th = _____
3rd = _____	8th = _____
4th = _____	9th = _____
5th = _____	10th = _____

Time of the day

9:00 = nine o'clock
10:15 = ten fifteen / a quarter past ten
11:30 = eleven thirty / half past eleven
12:45 = twelve forty-five / a quarter to one
14:50 = fourteen-fifty / ten to three

What's the time now?

It is

A _____

B _____

C _____

D _____

E _____

Prepositions of time

At steht bei Uhrzeiten: School starts **at** eight o'clock.

In steht bei längeren Zeiträumen: Your appointment is **in** May.

     bei Tageszeiten: The blood sugar test is **in** the morning.

                   The X-ray is **in** the afternoon.

On steht bei Tagen: Please come **on** Monday.

                        Your next appointment is **on** July 2nd.

The months of the year

Please translate

Januar	= *January*	Juli	= _____
Februar	= _____	August	= _____
März	= _____	September	= _____
April	= _____	Oktober	= _____
Mai	= _____	November	= _____
Juni	= _____	Dezember	= _____

The days of the week

Please translate

Montag	= _____
Dienstag	= _____
Mittwoch	= _____
Donnerstag	= _____
Freitag	= _____
Samstag	= _____
Sonntag	= _____

Would you like to play BINGO?

Just fill in the spaces with numbers from 1 to 50. The teacher will call out numbers. If the number is on your list, cross it out. The first person who has crossed out all numbers in a line, either horizontal, vertical or diagonal, calls out BINGO. He/she then reads out the numbers in the row. If the numbers are correct he/she is the winner.

1-10				
11-20				
21-30				
31-40				
41-50				

4.4 What does your body language tell about you?

Patients may be depressed or frightened. So it is very important to chat to them. Usually, it makes them more relaxed.

But it's not only what you say, it's also how you say it.
Assistants have a lot on their mind, and sometimes it's necessary to slow down and focus on how we are communicating.

Your body often shows what you think.
Unconsciously, it telegraphs your thoughts as you fold your arms, cross your legs, stand, walk, move your eyes and mouth. What does your body language tell your patients about you?

Keep arms, legs, and feet relaxed and uncrossed. Then patients think that you are open and honest.

Move within six to eight feet of your patient. Lean slightly forward. Interested people always pay attention and lean forward. Leaning backward demonstrates aloofness or rejection.

Pay attention to your patient's breathing and the pace that she or he is talking at. Is it fast or slow, then mirror them.

Direct eye contact is a compliment to most people and builds trust in you.

Your handshake should not be too hard and not too soft.

The style you use when speaking is as important as the words you choose.
If you speak hurriedly, the patient will come away with an impression that you were in a hurry, regardless of what you said.

Most people are unconscious of their body language, but it speaks volumes about what they are **really** thinking.

Body language guidelines:

Try to put on a decent smile.

Try not to speak in a sarcastic or accusatory tone.

Keep eye contact with the patient during communication.

What does the body language in each picture reveal? Point out the details.

4.5 Getting important information from the patient

Asking patients for their personal data

Assistant:	Good morning. Have you ever been treated here?
Patient:	*No, I haven't.*
Assistant:	Please tell me your first name and your family name.
Patient:	*My name is Jane Curtis.*
Assistant:	Would you mind spelling your name?
Patient:	*C-U-R-T-I-S, J-A-N-E.*
Assistant:	When were you born?
Patient:	*I was born on February 20, 1984.*
Assistant:	Are you a tourist or do you live here?
Patient:	*I am on holiday. At the moment I'm staying at the Miramar Hotel, Glockenstraße 11 in Bremen.*
Assistant:	What is your nationality?
Patient:	*I am Canadian.*
Assistant:	I see. In Germany, health insurances pay the fee for a treatment. There is no agreement with your country for paying the fee of your treatment. You'll have to pay for it.
Patient:	*I expected this. Do you take one of the usual credit cards: Visa or American Express?*
Assistant:	(laughs) I'm afraid that isn't possible. You will have to sign a payment obligation. Could I see your passport, please?
Patient:	*Certainly, here you are.*
Assistant:	Thank you. Would you please sign this.
Patient:	*Of course. Do you already know what I'll have to pay?*
Assistant:	I'm afraid I can't tell you in advance what the treatment will cost.
Patient:	*That's okay.*
Assistant:	Fine. Please take a seat in the waiting room. You'll have to wait for about half an hour.

Please label the file card

A file card (medical record) includes your medical history, results of physical examinations, reports of X-ray and laboratory tests, diagnosis and treatment plans.

It shows your symptoms, what tests were ordered, and how you responded to the treatment.

Today, computers replace the traditional paper record.

A	B	C	D	E	F	G	H	I	J	K	L	M	N	O	P	Q	R	S	Sch	St	T	U	V	W	X	Y	Z

Kartei-Nr. [ ]   M F R — P   Behandlungszeiträume

NAME:

FORENAME:

ADDRESS:

DATE OF BIRTH:

Please translate:

1. Patienten um ihre Personalien bitten: _____

2. Krankenversicherungen: _____

3. Gebühr für eine Behandlung bezahlen: _____

4. Zahlungsverpflichtung: _____

5. Karteikarte (2 Begriffe): _____

An emergency

An English student had an accident. You ask her for personal data. Tell her that she won't have to wait for a long time.

Please complete the dialogue.

Patient: I had an accident.

Assistant: What happened?

Patient: I think I've broken my arm. It hurts terribly when I try to move it.

Assistant: _____

Patient: _____

Assistant: _____

Patient: _____

Changing of personal data

An Irish friend of a family in Emden comes into the surgery. You already know her. She was treated last summer in the surgery because of an insect bite. The patient married two months ago, and so you have to change her name on the file card. Her name isn't Julia Brendell any more, but O'Connor. Family Augustin moved from Biegelstraße to Deichstraße in Emden. As the invoice has to be sent to their address, you have to change the address of Family Augustin as well: Deichstr. 27, 26721 Emden.

Please play the roles of doctor's assistant and patient at the reception.

Sarah – A New Patient

Anja:	*Guten Tag. Was kann ich für Sie tun?*
Sarah:	Emmh … do you speak English?
Anja:	*A little, yes. How can I help you?*
Sarah:	I would like to see the doctor, please.
Anja:	*Do you have an appointment?*
Sarah:	Well, … no, I don't. You see, I've been suffering from a pain in my chest since this morning.
Anja:	*Mmmh … let's see … we're very busy today. You'll have to wait.*
Sarah:	That's no problem.
Anja:	*Have you ever been here before?*
Sarah:	No, I haven't.
Anja:	*May I ask you to fill in the medical history form?*
Sarah:	Yes, of course. What do you want to know?
Anja:	*We need to know some facts about your previous health history.*
Sarah:	I see.
Anja:	*Do you have any history of heart trouble?*
Sarah:	Yes, I have a high blood pressure.
Anja:	*Do you take drugs regularly?*
Sarah:	Yes, I do. I take beta-blockers.
Anja:	*And have you got an allergy?*
Sarah:	No, I don't.
Anja:	*Have you got an infectious disease like AIDS or hepatitis?*
Sarah:	No, I don't.
Anja:	*May I ask you whether you are pregnant?*
Sarah:	Why do you want to know this?
Anja:	*Maybe we'll have to take an X-ray. During pregnancy, no X-rays should be taken.*
Sarah:	I see. No, I'm sure that I'm not pregnant.
Anja:	*Thank you very much. Oh, by the way … have you got a medical card from a German health insurance?*
Sarah:	No, I haven't.
Anja:	*Fine. So my colleague Janka will ask you for some personal details for our records.*
Sarah:	Sure.
Anja:	*Would you like to take a seat in the waiting room? – I'll call you when the doctor is ready to see you.*
Sarah:	Thank's a lot.

Pair-work 1

Imagine you were Janka. Ask Sarah for her personal details.
Prepare and act a dialogue.

Pair-work 2

Ask one of your classmates about her medical history.
Prepare and act a dialogue.

Individual work: Please translate the phrases into German.

Some useful questions to ask a patient:

1. What's wrong with you? _____

2. What's the trouble/problem? _____

3. What can I do for you? _____

4. Have you got a temperature? _____

5. Would you get undressed, please? _____

   Will you please take off your clothes? _____

   _____

Patients may answer:

1. I'm not feeling well. _____

2. I feel awful. _____

3. I've got a bad cold. _____

4. I've got an upset stomach. _____

5. I've got a heartburn. _____

6. I've got a headache. _____

7. I'm having trouble with my heart. _____

8. I've had a sore throat for the last two days. _____

9. I've been feeling feverish for one or two days. _____

10. I've got a mild pain. _____

11. I've got a severe pain. _____

12. I've got a piercing pain. _____

During the examination the doctor may say:

1. I'd like to examine you. _____

2. Stand up, please. _____

3. Please roll your sleeve up. _____

4. I'll just check your blood pressure/pulse. _____

5. Please lie down. _____

6. I'd like to listen to your chest. _____

7. Please take a deep breath. _____

8. Please hold your breath in. _____

9. Can you show me where the pain is?

   Can you show me where it hurts? _____

10. When did you first notice the pain? _____

11. Does it hurt when I move your leg? _____

12. Please turn around. _____

13. Would you open your mouth, please? _____

14. Put out your tongue, please. _____

15. Please say "Ah". _____

16. I'll arrange some tests for you. _____

17. We'll do a blood/urine test. _____

18. We'll do a blood picture. _____

19. We'll do a cancer check-up. _____

20. I'll give you an injection. _____

21. Have you taken anything for it? _____

Individual work: Please translate the phrases into German.

After the examination the patient may ask:

1. Is there anything seriously wrong, doctor? _____

   _____

2. Must I stay in bed? _____

3. Can I go to work tomorrow? _____

   _____

4. Could I get a sick note? _____

   _____

5. Do I need a prescription? _____

   _____

6. How often do I have to take the medicine? _____

   _____

The doctor may answer:

1. It's nothing serious. _____

2. You are suffering from high blood pressure. _____

   _____

3. You'll have to have an operation. _____

4. I'm going to send you to a hospital. _____

   _____

5. I'll have to refer you to a specialist for further treatment. _____

   _____

6. You don't have to stay in bed. _____

7. You'll have to stay in bed for a few days. _____

   _____

8. I'll prescribe you some pills. _____

9. I'll give you a prescription for a box of paracetamol. _____

   _____

10. You can get them at the chemist's. _____

    _____

11. You should take the tablets three times a day: _____

    _____

    in the morning, at noon and in the evening. _____

    _____

12. Take two tablespoonfuls of the drops. _____

    _____

13. Take the medicine before / during / after the meal. _____

    _____

14. The pills should be taken for a week. _____

15. You'll have to keep a strict diet. _____

16. No coffee, alcohol, cigarettes, and physical exertion. _____

    _____

17. I'd recommend you to avoid stress. _____

    _____

18. I hope you'll soon be better. _____

    _____

Please prepare and act dialogues.

1. You are in Edinburgh and suffer from a terrible cold and a sore throat.
   You have had a temperature for two days.
   You go to a doctor. The assistant asks you for your personal data and your medical history.
   The doctor examines you and tells you what to do. He prescribes some pills.

2. A tourist from Australia has had an upset stomach for two days. You ask her to describe her symptoms.
   The doctor examines her and tells her what to do.

3. An Irish owner of a pub in Berlin has got a piercing pain in his chest. You measure his blood pressure.
   Your boss prescribes him heart drops.
   They should be taken after the meals. The patient is told to avoid stress.
   He is referred to a specialist.

A toothache in Osnabrück

At the reception

Patient:	*Excuse me, do you speak English?*
Sylvia:	Yes, I do. What can I do for you?
Patient:	*My name is Brenda Stone. I'm spending my holidays here in Osnabrück.*
	I have a terrible toothache and I hope the dentist can see me.
Sylvia:	How long have you had it?
Patient:	*For two days.*
Sylvia:	Which tooth hurts?
Patient:	*I cannot tell you exactly which tooth hurts. The pain is in the upper jaw at the front.*
Sylvia:	Okay. Please go to treatment room 3.
Patient:	*Thank you very much.*
Sylvia:	You are welcome.

In the treatment room

Dentist:	Hallo, Miss Stone. Please come with me.
Patient:	*Hallo, Dr Brunner.*
Dentist:	My assistant Sylvia told me what kind of trouble you have. When does your tooth hurt?
Patient:	*The pain began when I was drinking coffee. Last night I couldn't sleep because of the steady pain.*
Dentist:	So let's have a look. Open your mouth, please. Does it hurt when I tap on this tooth?
Patient:	*No, it doesn't.*
Dentist:	What about this one?
Patient:	*Ouch!*
Dentist:	I am going to use this probe to check if you have caries. – Well, you have a cavity under this old composite filling. The filling and the decay must be removed.
Patient:	*Will it hurt?*
Dentist:	No, it won't. I am going to give you an injection. After that you'll have to wait for some minutes.
Patient:	*Fine.*
Dentist:	We'll also take an X-ray of your tooth.

After the X-ray

Dentist:	The pulp is so badly inflamed that it must be removed. Root canal treatment is the only way to save your tooth. Keep your mouth wide open, please. I'll put a temporary filling in your tooth today.
Patient:	*I'm happy the procedure is over now.*
Dentist:	Please take the glass, rinse your mouth and spit out. I want to see you tomorrow.
Patient:	*No problem. Oh, by the way, do you know where I could relax from all this stress?*
Dentist:	Why don't you visit Osnabrück's Altstadt and have a rest in a small coffee shop?
Patient:	*That's a good idea. See you tomorrow.*
Dentist:	Bye-bye.

Please answer the following questions on the dialogue:

1. What is Brenda's problem?
2. What does Brenda tell Sylvia about her toothache?
3. Does Dr Brunner have time for Brenda?
4. When did Brenda's toothache begin?
5. Why does Dr Brunner use a probe?
6. Where does Brenda have a cavity?
7. Why must the pulp be removed?
8. Where could Brenda relax from the stress she had at the dentist's?

Please play the roles of a patient and a dental assistant.

1. During a visit in Oxford you suddenly have a toothache. You ring a dentist, tell the dental assistant your problem, and make an appointment.
2. You arrive at the dentist's surgery and the dental assistant takes down your personal data (name, address, …).
3. Sitting in the dental chair, you tell the dentist which tooth hurts and that a filling has fallen out. He tells you there's a cavity which will have to be filled. The dentist wants to give you an injection.
4. A patient has a swollen cheek. It's his wisdom tooth that causes the problem. Tell the patient that his wisdom tooth is impacted and that it should be extracted as soon as possible.

Please find expressions and translate them into German

1. keep ······	filling	*1. keep your mouth open*	*halten Sie Ihren Mund geöffnet*
2. root canal	on a tooth		
3. wait	a probe		
4. to give	pain		
5. upper	room		
6. treatment	your mouth		
7. to take	decay		
8. steady	an X-ray		
9. to tap	jaw		
10. spit	an injection		
11. to use	for some minutes		
12. composite	a tooth		
13. to remove	your mouth open		
14. rinse	treatment		
15. to save	out		

4.6 Giving directions

Patient: *Excuse me, would you mind telling me the way to the toilet?*
Assistant: Turn left round the corner, please. The toilet is next to treatment room 2.
Patient: *Thank you.*

Please draw a plan of the surgery you work in. Then tell a patient how to get from the reception to the …

… toilet

… waiting room

… treatment room

… laboratory room

… X-ray room

… _____

… _____

Patient:	*Excuse me, can you tell me the way to the nearest pharmacy?*
Assistant:	Yes, certainly. You go out of the surgery, turn left and go along Lange Straße, until you come to a crossroads with traffic lights. There you turn right into Berliner Allee. You walk straight towards a blue building. That's Bären-Apotheke.
Patient:	*That's easy to find, I guess. Thank you very much for your information. Bye-bye.*
Assistant:	You're welcome. Bye-bye.
Patient:	*How can I get to the Albertinen-Krankenhaus?*
Assistant:	You should take the bus number 11 to Saarplatz. Turn left and walk to the end of the street. There you'll see a yellow sign saying „Albertinen-Krankenhaus".
Patient:	*Thank you for your help.*

4.7 Giving advice on products in the pharmacy

Selling an after-sun lotion in Goslar

Claudia:	Good morning. What can I do for you?
Customer:	*I'm sure you can help me. I'm spending my holidays here in the Harz mountains.*
Claudia:	Great. It's a wonderful day today, isn't it?
Customer:	*Yes, it is. It's almost as hot as in California.*
Claudia:	Do you come from California?
Customer:	*No, I'm from New York. As you can see, I'm a pale guy who has already caught a sunburn here in so-called „rainy Germany".*
Claudia:	Oh, that looks bad.
Customer:	*Can you recommend something for sunburn?*
Claudia:	Well, you've really overdone the sunbathing. You need to apply a good after-sun lotion. It will cool down your red skin and will give some moisture protection.
Customer:	*Will it really help to prevent my skin from peeling?*
Claudia:	I think so. You should use a sunscreen product with a high … Sonnenschutzfaktor.
Customer:	*You mean an SPF?*
Claudia:	Pardon. I didn't understand you. I'm just learning English at the vocational school. Could you explain what an SPF is?
Customer:	*I'll try. SPFs vary from country to country. American Sun Protection Factors tend to provide lower protection. Our SPF numbers are higher than yours. In America I use SPF 18.*
Claudia:	I think you should use SPF 20.
Customer:	*This would be almost SPF 40 in America. I could try this. It's a pity I always burn and rarely tan.*
Claudia:	Try this sunscreen. It's very good. Please make sure you apply it in a cool place to dry and clean skin. Damp skin will dilute the protection. Read the instructions carefully to see when you need to re-apply. By the way, wearing a hat also protects against sunbeams.
Customer:	*Thank you very much for your advice. How much is the lotion and the sunscreen product?*
Claudia:	It's 22 euros.
Customer:	*Here you are.*
Claudia:	Is there anything else I can do for you?
Customer:	*Yes, do you sell hats?*
Claudia:	No, but just around the corner there is a shop where you can get all kinds of hats. I wish you a nice holiday.
Customer:	*Thank you. Good-bye.*
Claudia:	Bye-bye.

Please fill in the missing words.

1. If someone has a _____ , he has spent too much time in hot sunshine.

2. If small pieces of skin are coming off your nose, you are _____ .

3. SPF means _____ .

4. If the sun has given your skin an attractive brown colour you have a _____ .

Comprehension – Please answer in complete sentences.

1. Is the customer male or female?
2. Why does Claudia recommend an after-sun lotion?
3. Explain what an SPF is.
4. Describe how to apply a sunscreen lotion.
5. What does the customer have to pay for the lotion and the sunscreen product?

How to pick the right sunscreen product:

Fair skin:
You are most at risk from the dangers of UV-light. You'll always burn. Use a sunblock or SPF 20. Protection is very important.

Allergy-prone skin:
You should use an unperfumed product. Do a patch test to be sure not to get an allergy. Your skin is very sensitive.

Normal-skin:
Take SPF 5 to 14. You should try a tinted sunscreen. You tan gradually to light brown.

Dark-skin:
Try SPF 2 to 4. The darker your skin, the less likely you are to burn. You tan to dark brown.

Please play the roles of a PKA and a customer.

1. A tourist from Ireland wants to have an after-sun lotion. Sell her a product.

2. You are spending your holidays in Miami Beach. In order to protect yourself from sunburn, you enter a drugstore and ask for a sunscreen product. The shop assistant recommends a cream which is good for your fair skin.

3. The suitcase of a London student did not arrive in Hannover, but in Tel Aviv. The student needs a toothbrush, toothpaste, a bottle of mouth-wash, nourishing cream and a bar of soap.

4. A soldier who works in your home town phones your pharmacy to ask whether his ointment has already been prepared. He wants to know when the pharmacy is open.

You can use the following phrases:
Can I help you?
What can I do for you?

I'd like something for a sunburn.
I need something for a sunburn.
I want something for a sunburn.

Could you give me ...?
Can I have ...?
Have you got ...?

DO YOU FIND SUNBATHING BORING?

Sunbathing is terrible. It leaves you red instead of golden brown. You can beautifully brown at home in a matter of hours with QUICKY-SELF-TAN. It reacts chemically with your skin. There is no risk of getting skin cancer. Even if it's raining non-stop, you will look like an Egyptian queen. Please remember to wash your hands thoroughly after application or you'll end up with them stained.

1. Please translate the advertisement for QUICKY-SELF-TAN.

2. Please create an advertisement for a sunscreen product or a self-tan product.

3. A tourist whom you sold a sunscreen product yesterday enters the pharmacy, complains about the product and wants to have his money back. He is dissatisfied with the product, because he developed an allergy.

Please write a dialogue between yourself and the customer.

4.8 Internet Research

Results for body language

BODY LANGUAGE

Nonverbal communication by means of facial expressions, eye behavior, gestures, posture, and other bodily signs. This form of language expresses emotions, feelings, and attitudes. Some non-verbal expressions are particular to certain cultures. Kinesics, the scientific study of body language, was pioneered by anthropologist Ray L. Birdwhistell, who wrote „Introduction to Kinesics" (1952).

Make an Internet Research in order to get more information about „body language" .
Use **www.google.com**

Group-work

Work in small groups of four to six students. Produce a wall-picture about body language at work.
You can take photos of typical situations, draw pictures or write scenes.
Present your products to the class and exhibit them at your vocational school.

Grammar Revision

Modal Auxiliaries (Modale Hilfsverben)

The patient	can	(kann)	
	could	(könnte)	
	may	(darf)	
	might	(dürfte)	
	will	(wird)	
	would	(würde)	
	should	(sollte)	stay in bed.
	ought to	(sollte)	
	must	(muss)	
	has to	(muss)	
	needn't	(braucht nicht)	
	mustn't	(darf nicht)	

Please translate:

1. Darf ich Ihnen helfen? _____

2. Ich kann nicht schlafen. _____

3. Würden Sie bitte Ihren
   Namen buchstabieren? _____

4. Sie sollten nicht rauchen. _____

5. Muss ich diese Medizin einnehmen? _____

6. Nein, das brauchen Sie nicht. _____

7. Sie dürfen nicht arbeiten. _____

8. Der Doktor wird Sie untersuchen. _____

9. Sie brauchen ein Rezept. _____

10. Könnte ich bitte
    einen Termin bekommen? _____

11. Warum soll ich
    schon so früh kommen? _____

Present Perfect

Present Perfect wird verwendet, wenn man ausdrücken will, seit wann oder wie lange ein Zustand (z. B. eine Krankheit, bestimmte Beschwerden) schon andauert.

Es wird gebildet aus **have/has + Past Participle**

Signalwörter sind:	**since**	**for**
	Zeitpunkt, an dem etwas begann:	Zeitraum:
	seit 10 Uhr	seit 3 Stunden
	seit gestern	seit 4 Tagen (4 Tage lang)
	seit meiner Kindheit	seit langem

Please translate:

1. Sie hat seit drei
Jahren hohen Blutdruck. _____

2. Er hat seit Mittwoch
starke Schmerzen. _____

3. Sie ist seit einer Stunde
im Behandlungsraum. _____

4. Das Kind fühlt sich
seit zwei Stunden fiebrig. _____

5. Der Patient
wartet seit elf Uhr. _____

Conditional Sentences (Bedingungssätze)

Im If-Satz wird die Bedingung genannt, im Hauptsatz wird die Folge (Konsequenz) angegeben.

Typ 1:   Es ist **sehr wahrscheinlich**, dass etwas passiert:

If you **give** me a kiss, I **will get** herpes.
Wenn Du mir einen Kuss gibst, werde ich Herpes bekommen.

Present Tense + Future I

Typ 2:   Es ist **gerade noch vorstellbar**, dass etwas passiert:

If you **gave** me a kiss, I **would get** herpes.
Wenn Du mir einen Kuss geben würdest, bekäme ich Herpes.

Past Tense + Conditional I

Typ 3:   Es ist **unmöglich** (zu spät), dass etwas passiert:

If you **had given** me a kiss, I **would have got** herpes.
Wenn Du mir einen Kuss gegeben hättest, hätte ich Herpes bekommen.

Past Perfect + Conditional II

Please translate:

1. Wenn Du die Tabletten nicht einnimmst, wirst Du krank.

_____

2. Wenn Du im Bett bleibst, wirst Du Dich bald viel besser fühlen.

_____

3. Wenn der Doktor mir ein Rezept gegeben hätte, wäre ich nicht 4 Wochen lang krank gewesen.

_____

4. Wenn ich ein Kondom benutzt hätte, würde ich nicht AIDS bekommen haben.

_____

5. Wenn ich die Pille nehme, werde ich nicht schwanger.

_____

6. Wenn Du Zahnschmerzen hättest, würdest Du zum Zahnarzt gehen.

_____

Please complete the sentences

1. If you gave me an appointment, I _____ (to come).

2. If he had told me about his problem, I _____ (to help) him.

3. If he doesn't see the doctor, he _____ (to die).

4. If I had a heart attack, I _____ (to phone) for a doctor.

5. If you had given me an injection, _____ I (to run) away.

6. If I had had a headache, I _____ (not to come) to the party.

7. If I were rich, I _____ (to travel) to Jamaica.

Please create three different types of conditional sentences and translate them into German.

Type 1: _____

_____

Type 2: _____

_____

Type 3: _____

_____

What do you know about certain diseases and their treatments?

5.1 Cancer

Lisa Cameron (22) and her sister Jenny (20) are sitting at the breakfast table.

Lisa: Jenny, I've got a big problem.

Jenny: *What's the matter, Lisa?*

Lisa: For two weeks, I've had a lump in my left breast. Oh, Jenny! I'm worried of having breast cancer.

Jenny: *I really understand your fear. Does the lump hurt?*

Lisa: No, it's painless.

Jenny: *This lump is a serious warning sign. It can be dangerous.*

Lisa: Some people think cancer is a death sentence.

Jenny: *It doesn't have to be cancer. Early detection may help people live much longer. If you have a malignant tumor, it will grow unless something is done to stop it.*

Lisa: You are right. I will see a doctor tomorrow.

Please complete the sentences with the correct word from the text.

1. You suffer from an illness or a _____ .

2. If you get better by taking pills you are _____ .

3. A small, hard thing in a breast is called a _____ .

4. If a lump does not hurt, it is _____ .

5. The English term for "Todesurteil" is _____ .

6. The English term for "Früherkennung" is _____ .

7. If a cancer is uncontrollable it is called _____ .

Please work in pairs: write a dialogue and act it with your partner. One of you is Lisa, the other one is a doctor's assistant.

Lisa comes to the doctor's assistant and tells her about her symptoms and her fear of having breast cancer. The assistant talks to her in a friendly way and tells her that the lump may be a harmless tumor. She talks to her about the possibility of having an operation to remove the tumor. Furthermore, she tells her that there are certain drugs which stop the growth of a tumor, the so-called cytotoxic drugs.

Brainstorming

Please write down a list of words which you associate with cancer.

_____ _____ _____

_____ _____ _____

_____ _____ _____

_____ _____ _____

Different forms of cancer

Blutkrebs	leukaemia	**Gehirntumor**	brain cancer
Brustkrebs	breast cancer	**Hautkrebs**	skin cancer
Darmkrebs	cancer of the rectum	**Lungenkrebs**	lung cancer
Gebärmutterkrebs	cancer of the uterus		

Do you know anyone who has cancer?
Please share your personal knowledge about this disease with the class.

Please fill in the type of cancer which is described.

1. _____ : The patient coughs blood and is short of breath.

   Smoking enhances the risk of getting it.

2. _____ : The patient suffers from headaches and feels dizzy.

   There are no obvious reasons why someone gets this type of cancer.

3. _____ : There is a sudden change in the size and the colour of a mole.

   At least 90 percent of this type of cancer is caused by the sun. One in every seven Americans gets it. It is completely curable if treated in its earliest stages.

4. _____ : There are periods of constipation and diarrhoea.

   A bad diet enhances the risk of getting this type of cancer.

5.2 Heart attack
Stroke

The most common causes of death among western people are heart disease and cancer. Heart disease is the number-one killer.

And what about you? Have you got a healthy heart?

Check which of the following statements apply to you.

Yes	No	
☐	☐	I have a family history of heart disease.
☐	☐	One of my parents/grandparents died of stroke/heart attack.
☐	☐	I've got high blood pressure.
☐	☐	I've got a high blood cholesterol level.
☐	☐	I smoke.
☐	☐	I weigh too much.
☐	☐	I do not get much exercise.
☐	☐	I've got a lot of stress in my life.
☐	☐	I take the pill.

How many risk factors apply to you?

If there are two or more please tell your classmates what you will change in your life in order to have a really long life.

Robert Springsteen lives in London. He is 36 years old and has a job as a manager. He usually works 12 hours a day. At the weekend he likes to play squash and tennis. Robert smokes about 40 to 60 cigarettes a day and likes hamburgers and chips.

Please give reasons why Robert Springsteen is very likely to catch a heart-disease.

At night, Robert suddenly woke up with a piercing pain in his chest. The pain went down his left arm. His wife was alarmed. She knew that time is important in treating a heart attack. The longer a patient waits before the treatment, the less chance he has of getting better. A heart attack occurs when a part of the heart is suddenly cut off from its oxygen supply by a clot (Blutgerinnsel) in a coronary artery. Drugs must be given that make the blood "thinner".

Comprehension – please answer in complete sentences.

1. What are the typical symptoms of a heart attack?
2. How can a doctor diagnose a heart attack?
3. When does a heart attack occur?
4. Why is it important for the patient to get drugs?

5.3   Diabetes

Please complete the text below with the correct word from the word list.

sugar, weak and tired (schwach und müde), insulin, thirsty, pancreas, diet, itches (juckt), urinate, blood, sugar substitutes (Zuckerersatzstoffe), injection, diabetic foodstuffs (Diabetikerernährungsmittel).

Ernest Hemingway and Elvis Presley had diabetes.

The _____ does not produce enough insulin. Therefore, the blood has too much _____ .

A _____ sugar test will tell you if you have it. These are the warning signs of the disease:

you have to _____ a lot (the kidneys want to get rid of the extra sugar);

you drink a lot, you are always _____;

you are feeling _____;

your skin _____.

The disease can be controlled by giving oneself an _____ of _____

every day. Patients must follow a strict _____. They have to avoid foods high in sugar and fat.

They eat chocolates and jam which are sweetened with _____.

You can buy _____ in pharmacies and supermarkets.

1. Do you know a patient who suffers from diabetes? Please share your personal knowledge about this disease with the class. How can a doctor's assistant help a diabetic?
2. If you work in a pharmacy you'll sometimes sell diabetic foodstuffs. Please act a dialogue with a partner: sell a diabetic jam to a customer.

5.4 Allergies

The sun is shining, flowers are blooming, summer is coming and everyone feels wonderful – except for the poor people who suffer from allergies.

Are **you** allergic to pollen, dust, strawberries, nickel, …?
Do **you** suffer from itchy, swollen and watering eyes?
Tell the class about your symptoms and the way your doctor treats the symptoms.

If you work at a dermatological surgery, please inform the class about further ways of helping a patient.

5.5 Headaches/Migraine

Pair-work

Have a look at the girl. Make up a little story about her. What do you think is the matter with her? Give reasons. Write about 100 words and say in which way you would help her.
Please present your texts to the class.

Talk to your partner and find out
- how often and when she suffers from headaches;
- what are the reasons for the pain;
- how she could prevent headaches.

In order not to get headaches do / don't do the following things:

Dos	Don'ts
1. _____	1. _____
2. _____	2. _____
3. _____	3. _____
4. _____	4. _____
5. _____	5. _____

5.6 Anorexia nervosa

Once upon a time there was a pretty girl of fourteen. Her name was Francesca. She went on a diet with some friends at school, because she wanted to look like the models you see in magazines and on TV. There was a lot of pressure on her to be slim. At that time Francesca weighed 55 kilos. She was ashamed of her body. Francesca felt unloved and unlovable. So she stopped eating.

5 Her mother seemed embarrassed when her periods started and when she had to buy her a bra. Francesca could not talk to her mother about her problems.

When she was sixteen, her father died. It was terrible for Francesca. She just didn't eat any more. Sometimes she tried to hide the food her mother gave her. She felt completely out of control about food. Francesca had extremely low self-esteem and she was dominated by her depressions and anger. She was sure she
10 was going to die.

Francesca weighed only 23 kilos when she was admitted into hospital. In hospital she was forced to eat. Slowly, she put on weight and got stronger. She started seeing a psychiatrist, whom she told how much she hated herself.

He told her that her disease was called anorexia nervosa. This disease is based on an emotional
15 problem, but it also has destructive physical effects. If it is not treated in time, organs can be damaged. The psychiatrist told Francesca that the disease is mainly found among young girls and that it is often called "the slimmer's disease". A girl starts it by dieting and then continues to lose more and more weight. By becoming thinner and thinner, the girl removes her sexual identity. She remains a child and so avoids the emotions that puberty bring. Illness, divorce or death in the family can be further causes of
20 anorexia nervosa.

Please match the terms with the definitions

1. pretty	**a.**	totally, absolutely
2. slim	**b.**	a piece of underwear for women
3. completely	**c.**	beautiful, good-looking
4. embarrassed	**d.**	to cause great damage
5. bra	**e.**	thin, well-shaped
6. to hide	**f.**	shy, ashamed
7. to force	**g.**	self-respect
8. destructive	**h.**	to put something in a place where it cannot be seen
9. divorce	**i.**	the formal ending of a marriage
10. self-esteem	**j.**	to make somebody do something, although he or she is unwilling to do it

1. What kind of problems did Francesca have within her family?
List a few typical ones.

2. What do you think were her reasons to stop eating?

3. What is typical for anorexia nervosa?

4. Francesca spent years wishing that she was perfect. What do you think she did after leaving the hospital? Please think of a possible continuation of her story. Write about 50–70 words.

5. Do you know a girl or a boy who suffers from anorexia nervosa or bulimia? Tell the class about the person.
(Bulimia is the drive to overeat, followed by self-indulged vomiting and/or laxative abuse = Bulimie ist eine Esssucht, gefolgt von selbst herbeigeführtem zügellosen Erbrechen, verbunden mit dem Missbrauch von Abführmitteln.)

5.7 Dementia / Alzheimer's Disease (AD)

My name is Rita. I am fifty years old. My mother Margret has dementia. That means that her brain cells are damaged. A head injury, stroke, brain tumor or disease (such as Alzheimer's Disease) can damage brain cells. So her brain does not work as properly as it should. Once brain cells have been destroyed, they cannot be replaced.

The trouble started when she forgot the names of her grandchildren. Tim and Sarah were really shocked on this Sunday afternoon. Weeks later she was looking for her purse. She found it in the refrigerator. My mum became totally confused about things and persons. She had trouble remembering recent events like the death of her sister. My mum lost interest in cooking and reading, two activities that were always so important to her.

She felt sad, lonely and worried.

At first we just thought that she was getting old, but we had to realize that Alzheimer's is not a process of aging but a disease which destroys a person`s identity.

My mother could not look after herself anymore. She neglected her personal hygiene and did not care if she brushed her teeth or not. So she needed help with washing, combing, dressing, and eating. She asked the same questions again and again. She did not know whether it was Friday or Monday. Two hours after lunch she asked me what she would get for lunch.

Caring for someone with dementia is very difficult. Sometimes I am totally exhausted. At the age of 75 she is like a child. Sometimes she even reacts in an aggressive way, even to Tim and Sarah. They are afraid of their grandmother. Last week she wandered away from home and was found in a supermarket. The problem was that she went out in her nightdress. She is so confused.

Our doctor says that no treatment can stop AD. Of course there are tablets which may help prevent some symptoms from becoming worse for a limited time. They help against sleeplessness, depression, anxiety and agitation.

AD is named after Dr. Alois Alzheimer, a German doctor. In 1906 he found abnormal clumps (amyloid plaques) in the brain of a patient who had died of an unusual mental illness.

Should we take my mother to an old people`s home? Will she get there the total care she needs? I don't know whether the disease will progress slowly or rapidly. I feel helpless as well.

Please translate the text into German.

Demenz/Alzheimer Krankheit (AK)

Mein Name ist Rita …

List the symptoms of dementia which can be found in the story.

_____

_____

_____

▢ Imagine you found Margret in the supermarket. Write a dialogue between you and her.
▢ Do you know people who suffer from dementia? Tell the class about their problems.
▢ Write a dialogue between Margret and her daughter Rita.

To get more information about dementia use a search engine such as google.com

5.8 Parkinson's Disease (PD)

My name is Richard. I am 74 years old and live in an old people's home near Münster. I am a victim of Parkinson's Disease. What does this mean? Parkinson's Disease is a disorder that causes a progressive loss of nerve cell function in the part of the brain that controls muscle movement. Progressive means that you will lose more of your nerve function as time goes on.

My arms and legs tremble. I am not able to pour coffee into my mug. I can't accept the situation because I feel so helpless. I often feel depressed and don't want to meet other people. So I stay in front of the television all day and don't get out. I have to take the drug levodopa.

With Parkinson's, it is important to keep yourself physically and mentally active. So I get physiotherapy and chat with relatives and friends.

List the symptoms of PD which can be found in the text.

_____

_____

_____

_____

_____

_____

Richard asks for your help by writing a letter to Michael Burns, a man he met during World War II. He wants to tell him about his life and his disease. Help him write this letter and present it to the class.

Jonas (10), Richard's grandson, wants to have his grandfather back at home. He offers his parents to share his room with him and to help him with everything.

Write a dialogue between Jonas and his parents. Find arguments why Richard should stay in the old people's home or why it would be good for him to come home.

5.9 Internet Research

For general information about certain diseases use **www.webcrawler.com**. Go to the web site of health. You find medical diseases from A to Z and symptoms from A to Z.

In **www.netdoctor.co.uk** you can watch videos about healthy living and find a medical encyclopaedia.

In **www.healthfinder.gov** you find keywords on health from A to Z and interactive tools like health checkups, calculation of your body mass index as well as videos on wellness topics.

Group-work

The class is divided into groups of four students. Each group chooses one of the diseases which are presented in Unit 5 and conducts research on the internet. Dictionaries should be available in the classroom. You can also use an online-dictionary like **www.leo.org**. Each group produces a leaflet giving information about symptoms, diagnosis and treatment of the disease. You may cut out pictures from German health magazines. You may also try to get English health magazines.

Present the leaflets to the class and exhibit them at your vocational school.

You can get information on diseases and prevention on the following websites, but there are a great number of further websites you can discover:

www.womenshealth.gov about heart disease and prevention
www.cancer.org about the different types of cancer
www.stroke.org about stroke symptoms, women and stroke, kids and stroke
www.childrenwithdiabetes.com
www.diabetes.org about nutrition and fitness
www.verywell.com about food allergies, drug and latex allergies
www.parkinson.org search for personal stories and present them to the class
www.dementia.com you can find information on dementia and Alzheimer's

Grammar Revision

Direct and Reported Speech

Die indirekte Rede (reported speech) wird verwendet, wenn jemand erzählt, was ein anderer geschrieben, gesagt oder gefragt hat.

In Ihrem Beruf benötigen Sie die indirekte Rede z. B. dann, wenn Sie Ihrem Chef erzählen wollen, was ein Patient Ihnen berichtet hat.

Die indirekte Rede eignet sich aber auch vorzüglich zur Weitergabe von Klatsch und Gerüchten.

Grundprinzip zur Umwandlung von Sätzen in die indirekte Rede ist die Rückverschiebung: Das Verb wird im Satz der indirekten Rede um eine Zeitstufe in die Vergangenheit gerückt.

Direct Speech (Direkte Rede)	Reported Speech (Indirekte Rede)
Monika said:	You say …
I **work** in a pharmacy. **Present Tense** ·················▶	Monika said (that) she **worked** in a pharmacy. **Past Tense**
I **have worked** in a pharmacy for six months. **Present Perfect** ·················▶	Monika said (that) she **had worked** in a pharmacy for six months. **Past Perfect**
I **worked** in a pharmacy last year. **Past Tense** ·················▶	Monika said (that) she **had worked** in a pharmacy last year. **Past Perfect**
I **had worked** in a pharmacy. **Past Perfect** ·················▶	Monika said (that) she **had worked** in a pharmacy. **Past Perfect**
I **will work** in a pharmacy. **Future I** ·················▶	Monika said (that) she **would work** in a pharmacy. **Conditional I**
I **will have worked** in a pharmacy. **Future II** ·················▶	Monika said (that) she **would have worked** in a pharmacy. **Conditional II**
I **would work** in a pharmacy. **Conditional I** ·················▶	Monika said (that) she **would work** in a pharmacy. **Conditional I**
I **would have worked** in a pharmacy. **Conditional II** ·················▶	Monika said (that) she **would have worked** in a pharmacy. **Conditional II**

Please put the following statements into reported speech.

1. I have an appointment at 8.30. The patient said (that) he _____ an appointment at 8.30.

2. I live in Hannover. The patient said (that) _____.

3. Tom had an accident. My friend told me (that) _____ an accident.

4. I am interested in medicine. Julia said (that) _____ interested in medicine.

5. I haven't got high blood pressure. The patient said (that) he

   _____.

6. You can use our telephone. The doctor's assistant told me (that)

   _____.

Please transform into reported speech according to the example:

1. The patient said: I have got a lump in my left breast.

The patient told me (that) ————————————————————————————.

2. Mr. Swan said: I don't get much exercise.

Mr. Swan told me (that) ————————————————————————————.

3. My friend Tanja said: I take the pill.

My friend Tanja told me (that) ————————————————————————.

4. Mrs. Sullivan said: My husband had a stroke.

Mrs. Sullivan told me (that) ——————————————————————————.

5. Sonja said: I will marry a rich man.

Sonja told me (that) ——————————————————————————————.

6. The doctor said: Your disease is called anorexia nervosa.

The doctor told me (that) ————————————————————————————.

The Comparison (Die Arten der Steigerung)

Die meisten **einsilbigen** und alle **zweisilbigen Adjektive, die auf -er, -ow-, -le** und **-y enden**, werden mit **-er/-est gesteigert**.

old – older – oldest · pretty – prettier – prettiest

fat – fatter – fattest · happy – happier – happiest

Einige Adjektive haben **unregelmäßige Steigerungsformen**:

good – better – best · bad – worse – worst

many – more – most · much – more – most

Alle **mehrsilbigen Adjektive** werden mit **more/most** gesteigert:

interesting – more interesting – most interesting

difficult – more difficult – most difficult

dangerous – more dangerous – most dangerous

beautiful – more beautiful – most beautiful

Vergleiche werden folgendermaßen angestellt:

Anke is **older than** her sister.

Anke ist **älter als** ihre Schwester.

Anke is **not as old as** her sister.

Anke ist **nicht so alt wie** ihre Schwester.

Anke is **as old as** her sister.

Anke ist **so alt wie** ihre Schwester.

The older Anke gets, **the more beautiful** she looks.

Je älter Anke wird, **desto schöner** sieht sie aus.

Please translate:

1. Melanie ist glücklicher als Nicole.

——

2. Heute fühle ich mich viel schlechter als gestern.

——

3. Dieses Medikament ist teurer als das letzte.

——

4. Ich verdiene mehr Geld als du.

——

5. Sie ist so krank wie sie aussieht.

——

6. Die Operation war schwieriger als ich dachte.

——

7. Je mehr Kopfschmerzen ich habe, desto mehr Tabletten nehme ich.

——

8. Frischer Orangensaft schmeckt besser als Wasser.

——

9. Die neue Auszubildende ist so jung wie wir.

——

What can be done to prevent diseases?

6.1 Keeping fit and healthy

Please take "72" and calculate

If you are a woman, add (addiere) 3
If you are a man, subtract (subtrahiere) 3
If you live in a big city
   (over 1 million inhabitants), subtract 2
5 If you live in a village or in a small town, add 2
If any of your grandmothers and grandfathers
   lived to 80, add 2
If all four grandparents reached 80, add 6
If your father or mother died of stroke or heart attack
10   before the age of 50, subtract 4
If your father or mother, brother or sister has had cancer,
   heart disease or diabetes since childhood, subtract 3
If you live in your parents' house, add 1
If you live in a shared flat, subtract 1
15 If you live with a boyfriend or girlfriend, add 2
If you are happy, add 1
If you are unhappy, subtract 2
If you are overweight by 50 pounds or more, subtract 8
If you are overweight by 30 to 50 pounds, subtract 4
20 If you are overweight by 10 to 30 pounds, subtract 2
If you see the doctor for a check-up once a year, add 2
If you are between 20 and 30, add 1
If you work behind a desk, subtract 2
If you do hard physical work, add 2
25 If you exercise (tennis, jogging, . . .) once a week, add 2, twice a week, add 4
If you go to work by car, bus or train, subtract 2
If you go to work by bike, add 2
If you watch TV more than three hours a day, subtract 1
If you sleep less than 6 hours a day, subtract 2
30 If you sleep more than 10 hours each night, subtract 4
If you are often aggressive and ill-tempered (launisch), subtract 2
If you are relaxed (locker und entspannt), add 3
If you smoke more than 2 packs a day, subtract 8
If you smoke 1 to 2 packs a day, subtract 6
35 If you smoke 1/2 to 1 pack a day, subtract 3
If you drink alcohol daily, subtract 4
If you drink alcohol once or twice a week, subtract 2

Please add up your score (Punktestand) in order to know how long you may live according to this questionnaire.

What is really important for you in order to keep healthy and to enjoy life?
Please write about 60–80 words.

Exercise protects the heart. Studies have shown that lack of regular physical activity may be an even more important heart-disease risk factor than smoking or high blood pressure. Fitness can be fun in many ways. Do something regularly to improve your fitness. Sports should take place outside in healthy fresh air.

Please complete the table by choosing at least four of the following activities. You can try to find further aspects which are important for your life.

Activities:

swimming, dancing, stress, jogging, eating junk food (hot-dogs, hamburgers), windsurfing, watching TV, drinking alcohol, phoning someone, riding a bike, playing squash, going shopping, being on my own, being with my friends, smoking, eating sweets, going to the cinema, spending time with the family, cooking, dieting to keep my weight down …

I get fit and healthy by …	Bad for my health is …
I enjoy, like …	I hate, dislike, avoid …

6.2 Stress and some of its causes

People react differently to stress. For some of them, stress can be enjoyable and exciting. For others, it is the reason for severe diseases. There are many facts which can create stress: misunderstandings in the family, arguments at work, noise, having to work overtime, being under pressure (the phone is ringing, the boss wants to see the patient, …), contradictory instructions from colleagues, …

Please translate the text about stress.

Stress, und einige seiner Ursachen.

Die Menschen reagieren …

_____

_____

_____

_____

_____

The following list was developed by American doctors. A score of 160 or more is an indicator for a stressful life.

Death of husband or wife	100		Major change at work	39
Divorce	73		Money problems	38
Jail sentence	63		Child leaves home	29
Death of close relative	63		Starting/leaving school	26
Illness/injury	53		Moving	26
Marriage	50		Trouble with employer	23
Loss of job	47		Change in eating habits	15
Pregnancy	40		Christmas	12
Sex problems	39			

Stress makes the body fight or run away. If stress occurs repeatedly over a long period of time, you are in danger of losing your health.

Please find the correct pairs.

Did you find all pairs?

1. Verletzung _____ *injury* _____

2. Arbeitgeber _____

3. Gefängnisstrafe _____

4. Verwandte _____

5. Schwangerschaft _____

6. umziehen _____

7. beeinflussen _____

Work in small groups:

Please decide on a top ten of stress factors in your daily lives. Score them from one to ten. Compare your top ten list with those of the other groups.

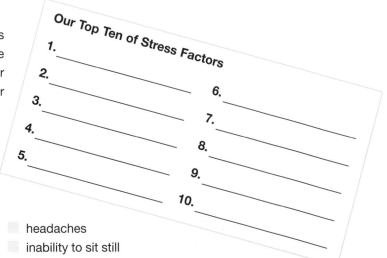

Our Top Ten of Stress Factors

1. _____
2. _____
3. _____
4. _____
5. _____
6. _____
7. _____
8. _____
9. _____
10. _____

Typical signs of stress:

- heartburn
- constipation/diarrhoea
- sleeplessness and tiredness
- nail biting
- difficulty in concentrating
- headaches
- inability to sit still

The longer you ignore the symptoms, the harder it will be to get rid of them.

Write a short essay about what you could do to avoid, reduce or cope with stress.

The Healing Power of Pets

Robert Turner is on his way to St. Martin's old people's home in Winchester. He is not alone, but has his two toy poodles in his arms. Monty and Gino will bring joy to the residents, of whom some suffer from depression and loneliness.

Several studies have shown that regular contact with pets can heal patients and even heart attack-patients get better quicker with the help of a dog or a cat. And so Robert visits the old people's home every Friday afternoon. He is one of several citizens of Winchester who supports the local health visitors, understanding his visits as his contribution to help people in need.

The residents are always very happy to see the cute poodles. Within minutes you can hear laughter in the home's day room of St. Martin's. Lucy Chatsworth takes Monty on her lap and strikes him gently. "My daughter Sally lives near Glasgow and she can only visit me once a month. I love having Monty here. It's so much better than watching television or listening to music. And his fur is so soft. Yes, I sometimes feel lonely and I'm looking forward to the Friday afternoons when Robert comes with his dogs."

And as the pet therapy is an acknowledged form of healing patients in other countries where pets are prescribed for therapy, Robert is surely on the right way.

Walking the Dog – How Far?

How much exercise does your dog need? That depends on its breed, and the state of its health. But that doesn't mean you have to walk your dog as far as possible, too. If you have a fenced area where your dog can exercise, it may easily cover the distance by itself, just running back and forth. Of course, if you do decide to exercise with your dog, you'll both benefit.

In which way can pets improve their owners' health?

1. _They are good companions so that people don't feel lonely._
2. _____
3. _____
4. _____
5. _____
6. _____
7. _____
8. _____

Please translate the two texts. You may use a dictionary.

Die heilende Kraft von Haustieren

Robert Turner ist auf seinem Weg zum ...

Wie lange und wie weit sollten Sie mit Ihrem Hund ausgehen?

Wie viel Bewegung braucht Ihr Hund? ...

Easing tension

There are some simple ways of easing tension, which take only a few minutes. The easiest way to relax before you go to bed is to have a warm bath and a warm glass of milk with honey. Even a glass of beer may lead you to sleep. Sleep is an excellent treatment for stress. Do **you** get enough of it? Try counting sheep. It helps the mind switch off after a busy day under stress in the surgery. There are also simple ways to relax your mind during a day at work. Close your eyes and imagine a pleasant peaceful scene … perhaps an idyllic place beneath a tree or a white beach in sunshine. Try to hear the sounds (birds, leaves in the wind, waves) and smell the scents (grass, flowers, salt, suncream). Put yourself in that scene.

Try to notice all that's around you: the blue sky, the feeling of sand between your toes, the warmth of the sun. A few minutes' daydreaming will relax and refresh you, and allow you to clear your mind and cope with stress more easily. Try to develop inner peace.

Be positive:

Turn a frustrating situation to your advantage. Be kind to yourself: an evening out after working hard, a new lipstick after a quarrel. Optimists are healthier. Pessimism may have a negative effect on the immune system. Learn to say "no" and mean it. Plan ahead. Take help from others if you feel you can't cope with stress.

Please decide whether the following sentences are true or false:

	true	false
1. Toes are the five parts at the end of your hands.	❏	❏
2. A scent is a pleasant smell.	❏	❏
3. Relaxing means working hard.	❏	❏
4. To switch off is in German „einschalten".	❏	❏
5. Tension is the feeling of nervousness.	❏	❏
6. If you cope with stress, you are able to manage it.	❏	❏
7. A benefit is something that is bad for your life.	❏	❏
8. If you ease tension, you reduce it.	❏	❏

If the sentence is false, please write the correct sentence in your exercise book.

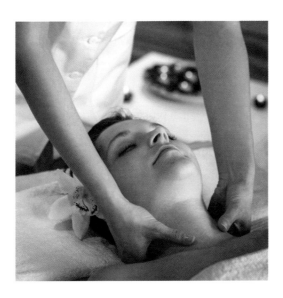

6.3 What to do when you are blue?

*Load up on
linguine … sleep
a little less …
start thinking happy
(and your mood will follow!).*

Like happiness, a certain amount of sadness is natural. When we lose a job or someone we love, it's normal to feel sad.

But when the sadness doesn't go away, when you feel down all the time, and maybe even think of ending it all … that's depression.

Depression weakens your immune system's ability to fight off disease.

The good news is that you can climb out of depression:

Enjoy pasta …

Pasta, rice and potatoes with their complex carbohydrates may lift you out of depression by boosting levels of the mood-stabilizing chemical serotonin.

Hide sugar and coffee …

A study at Texas A&M University proved that the moods of tested persons were better when they hadn't drunk coffee and eaten sugar.

Stay up past your bedtime …

Don't laugh. Even a few hours of sleep deprivation may improve your mood.

Set your alarm clock for earlier …

Try getting up a couple of hours earlier, and your mood may be better.

Distract yourself …

Fill your time with activities that will distract you from your negative thoughts. Depressed people who simply sit and ruminate about how sad they are tend to stay depressed longer than people who plan positive changes.

Start moving. Exercise can improve your mood.

Talk to your doctor …

Your depression might be caused by a physical problem – a side effect of a drug, premenstrual syndrome or a hormone disturbance.

Just say "STOP" to discouraging thoughts …

The idea is that you can truly make yourself miserable by thinking miserable or pessimistic thoughts. So try to think positive.

Pair-work

1. Write down four words you two would use to describe the feeling of being blue.

2. Ask your partner what she would do if feeling blue.

3. Present your results to the class.

6.4 Preventing caries and gingivitis

Decaying teeth are extremely painful. They cause bad breath and are unattractive to look at. Caries and gum disease can be prevented by following a simple daily routine of cleaning.

Alice is a 16-year-old patient, who asks Irina, a dental assistant, about possibilities of preventing caries.

Alice: How often should I brush my teeth?

Irina: *Brush after breakfast and before going to bed. When you are sleeping, the bacteria inside your mouth are wide awake. If you don't brush your teeth before you go to sleep, these bacteria will have an all-night party with the sugar and the plaque in your mouth. While you are dreaming, the acids destroy your teeth and there may be a hole.*

Alice: I brush my teeth twice a day. But I always brushed before breakfast, because I wanted to get rid of the bad taste in my mouth. How long should I brush my teeth?

Irina: *Brush your teeth for at least three minutes. By the way, what sort of toothbrush do you use?*

Alice: I use one with hard bristles, but my gums bleed very often.

Irina: *You shouldn't use hard bristles. My boss told me that you didn't remove your plaque very effectively. There was a lot of plaque around and underneath the gum margin, which got hard and rough. This substance is called tartar. It is the cause for bleeding and gingivitis.*

Alice: What kind of toothbrush do you recommend?

Irina: *It is very important that you use the right toothbrush. Take a medium nylon brush. It's wrong to think that hard bristles clean your teeth thoroughly. They may actually hurt your gums. Select a brush with a small flat head. The bristles of the brush should be rounded.*

Please translate:

1. kariöse, zerfallene Zähne _____

2. Zahnfleischerkrankung _____

3. Säuren _____

4. wenigstens _____

5. Borsten _____

6. mein Zahnfleisch _____

7. unterhalb _____

8. der Zahnfleischrand _____

9. Zahnstein _____

10. Zahnfleischentzündung _____

11. Zahnbürste _____

12. empfehlen _____

13. kleiner, ebener Kopf _____

Alice:	How often should I replace my toothbrush?
Irina:	*You should replace it every three months.*
Alice:	Do you recommend an electric toothbrush?
Irina:	*Electric toothbrushes may help handicapped people and may motivate you to brush your teeth. I think they are good for children.*
Alice:	What kind of toothpaste should I use?
Irina:	*Choose a toothpaste that contains fluoride. Be careful with toothpastes which promise wonders. You can't get snow-white teeth by only using a special toothpaste.*
Alice:	Why is it important to have fluoride in the toothpaste?
Irina:	*Fluoride strengthens the enamel and makes it more resistant to acids. Children are given fluoride drops from six months until all the permanent teeth other than the wisdom teeth have appeared – which is usually by about the age of 14. It can also be given in the form of a gel.*
Alice:	What else can I do to protect my teeth?
Irina:	*You should clean in-between your teeth. For this you can use dental floss or an interproximal brush. An interproximal brush is useful for cleaning large gaps.*

Please explain in your own words:

1. to replace: _____

2. handicapped people: _____

3. to protect: _____

4. dental floss: _____

Alice:	How should I brush my teeth?
Irina:	*There is no single, correct way of brushing. Brushing should be firm, but do not scrub. Aim the brush at a 45 degree angle, placing the bristles in the spaces between the teeth and gums, and brush gently in short circular strokes, covering only two or three teeth at a time. Start with the back teeth and brush the outside surface, working your way around the mouth to the other side. Repeat the same action on the back surface of each of the teeth. Finally, brush the biting surfaces.*
Alice:	How often should I see a dentist for a check-up?
Irina:	*You should see a dentist every six months.*
Alice:	Thank you very much for your help.
Irina:	*You are welcome.*

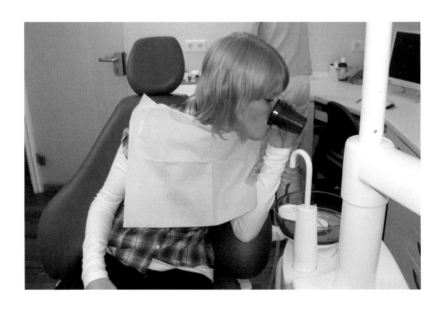

Please play the roles of a dental assistant and

- Linda, a 13-year-old girl, who likes to eat chocolate bars in bed after having brushed her teeth. Explain to her why this behaviour is bad for her teeth. Try to be psychologically clever.
- Mirinda, an 18-year-old student, who wants to know what kind of toothbrush and toothpaste she should use.
- Mrs Menke, a 36-year-old teacher, who wants to brush her teeth in a more effective way.

Please describe the picture

Which expressions do not belong to the groups? Please cross them out.

1. caries – cancer – gingivitis – tartar

2. bacteria – sugar – bristles – teeth – acids

3. bristles – head – nylon – rough

4. to avoid – to select – to choose – to take

5. fluoride – enamel – scrub – toothpaste

6. dental floss – fluoride – interproximal brush – toothbrush

7. to brush – to clean – to destroy – to free from dirt

8. gingivitis – gum disease – toothache – gum margin

A new method to prevent caries is to seal the fissures with a type of tough transparent plastic coat, soon after a permanent side tooth is through. This method is called fissure sealing.

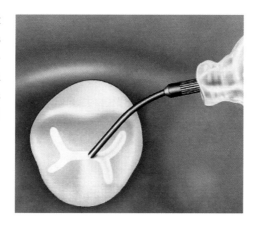

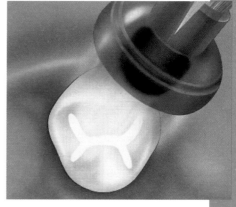

Please decide whether the following sentences are true or false!

	true	false
1. You should brush your teeth before breakfast.	❏	❏
2. Caries is caused by acids.	❏	❏
3. You should use a toothbrush with hard bristles.	❏	❏
4. Tartar is the cause for bleeding and gingivitis.	❏	❏
5. Your toothbrush should have a large head.	❏	❏
6. You should replace your toothbrush every eight months.	❏	❏
7. Your toothpaste should contain fluoride.	❏	❏
8. If you have a good toothbrush, you don't have to floss.	❏	❏
9. You should see a dentist once a year.	❏	❏

Are you a super patient and go to the dentist regularly?
Write about 60 to 80 words about what you do to prevent caries.

6.5 Preventing skin diseases

The skin is a barrier against microorganisms. It has sensors that feel touch, pressure, and pain. It's also important for the water balance and the body temperature. This is why we sweat. Sweat itself does not smell. The smell comes from bacteria on the skin.
Good skin is often a sign of good health.

5   People usually get acne during their teenage years, but adults can also get it. It may be a result of rising hormone levels, of stress and emotional problems. Even food which is high in fat can cause acne. Oily skin can be a problem. It should be washed twice a day with soap and warm water. Keep your skin clean and avoid fatty foods and make-up that has an oily base. Always use a clean towel. You should not squeeze spots. If you have a bad spot, dab it with a cotton bud soaked in lemon juice. Consult your doctor about
10 medications. Acne is aggravated by sunlight, heat, stress and spicy food. Teenage acne usually disappears in the early twenties.

Please translate:

1. ein Handtuch   _____

2. Pickel ausdrücken   _____

3. verschlimmert werden durch _____

4. gewürzte Speisen   _____

Please play the roles of a doctor's assistant and Gissa, a 15-year-old acne patient. She wants to know how to prevent spots and how to treat them.

Two women reveal their skin care secrets:

22-year-old Claire who works in a disco:
"My skin has to cope with smoke, lots of late nights and long hours. It's oily and until recently I had a lot of spots. For three months I have used a moisturiser. This lotion protects and softens my skin and stops it from becoming too dry. I eat plenty of fresh fruit and vegetables and drink a lot of water. I avoid sweets and I also avoid sunlight. In former times I spent hours and hours sunbathing, but now I don't stay in the sun for long. The skin wrinkles and I'm afraid of looking old. If you get a sunburn very often you are likely to get skin cancer."

21-year-old Rosa who is an aerobic teacher:
"Two years ago, I took a shower four times a day, until I made my skin totally dry and red. Today, I don't use any soap, but a cleansing gel from the pharmacy, which refreshes me all over. My skin needs special care. It should be kept clean, but it shouldn't be washed too often with soap, because soap dries the skin. Therefore, I have a shower only once every two days. I use a skin moisturer several times a day. I don't buy products for my skin in a supermarket anymore. Trying lots of different products made the problem worse. Pharmacy skincare is more expensive, but my skin is worth the extra money. I can recommend hypoallergenic products. They contain only pure ingredients which don't irritate the skin."

Please work in pairs. Translate either Claire's or Rosa's text into German. You may use a dictionary.

Die 22-jährige Claire, die in einer Disco arbeitet:
„Meine Haut muss Rauch, …

Die 21-jährige Aerobiclehrerin Rosa:
„Vor zwei Jahren habe ich vier Mal am Tag geduscht, …

Claire and Rosa told you about their skin problems. What was bad and what was good for their skin? Please fill in the table.

Bad	Good

You might want to try a face mask which is relaxing for you and your skin. Here are some recipes:

Home-made face masks

For dry skin:
Mix together a tablespoon of plain yogurt, a teaspoon of runny honey and a mashed, ripe avocado. Spread the mixture on your face and leave it on for ten to fifteen minutes.

For oily skin:
Mix together a tablespoon of plain yogurt, a teaspoon of honey, a teaspoon of oatmeal and a mashed peach. Spread it on your face and leave it on for ten minutes.

For normal skin:
Crush a few thick slices of cucumber to a pulp and mix them with a teaspoon of plain yogurt and a few drops of rose water. Spread the mixture on your face and leave it on for fifteen minutes.

6.6 Preventing infectious diseases

Have you ever wondered what it was like to live in the days before the discovery of vaccination? Infectious diseases killed millions of people every year throughout the world. Feared diseases in former times were the bubonic plague (Beulenpest), tuberculosis, and smallpox (Pocken).

Nowadays, in developed countries, these diseases kill only few people. One of the main reasons for this is the use of vaccines, which can protect us against many infectious diseases. The first vaccination was carried out against smallpox in 1976 by Dr Edward Jenner.

Vaccines are produced from the bacteria or viruses that cause the disease. The bacteria or viruses are made harmless or killed in the laboratory. Vaccines are injected into the body. A vaccine causes a very mild form of the disease. To protect itself, the body produces antibodies and the person becomes immune to the disease. Bacteria or viruses are destroyed, but the antibodies remain. After two or three injections you have enough antibodies to protect you for several years. After a few years it may be necessary to have a booster injection.

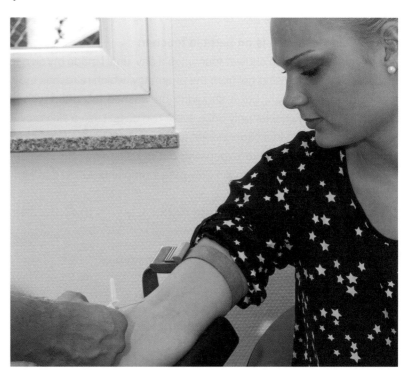

Wichtige Impfungen

polio	Kinderlähmung	**tetanus**	Tetanus/Wundstarrkrampf
whooping cough	Keuchhusten	**diphteria**	Diphterie
measles	Masern	**tuberculosis**	Tuberkulose
rubella	Röteln	**hepatitis B**	Hepatitis B/Leberentzündung
chicken-pox	Windpocken		

Facts about rabies

Vaccinated dogs or cats are protected against rabies if bitten by an infected animal. An infected animal sits with its mouth hanging open, perhaps with saliva dropping from its mouth. It may snap at imaginary objects. A cat may scratch for no apparent reason. Every pet with rabies shows a personality change. A quiet animal may become aggressive. An aggressive animal may suddenly be loving. Take your pet to a veterinarian immediately if it is bitten by a wild animal, or if you suspect it may have rabies.

Please translate the text about rabies

Fakten über Tollwut

Geimpfte Hunde oder Katzen …

Have you ever seen an animal with rabies? Please tell the class about it.

Please fill in the names of the diseases.

rubella; cholera; tetanus; tuberculosis; food poisoning; common cold; hepatitis B; influenza

1. _____ is a main killer in poorer parts of the world. You can get it by drinking contaminated water or eating contaminated food. You get fever, diarrhoea and severe thirst. Overcrowding,
poverty, and dirty water are ideal conditions for this disease.

2. _____ is caused by bacteria which slowly destroy the lung. The symptoms include
coughing, spitting, and general weakness.

3. A _____ and _____ are caused by viruses, which spread easily
because they can travel in the tiny droplets of moisture which we all pass out when we sneeze. You have
a runny nose, a sore throat, and a headache. You feel tired. You should use paper tissues and keep away
from other people. Rest and drink hot liquids. Take over-the-counter drugs like nose drops, cough sirup,
and aspirin. Take vitamin C. It may reduce the length of this disease. Rub an ointment onto your chest
and inhale etheric oils like camphor or menthol. This will bring relief.

4. _____ is caused by a virus. The virus causes serious damage to embryos during the
first three months of pregnancy.

5. _____ is caused by a bacterium. It attacks the nerves and may cause paralysis or
death. Spores which are in the soil can get into dirty cuts. Anyone with a deep and dirty cut should
always be vaccinated against it.

6. _____ is caused by bacteria called salmonella. These bacteria grow rapidly in luke-
warm food. You should always leave dishes in cool places, and don't reheat meals more than once. A
temperature of 95° C kills salmonella. Be careful with chicken and eggs. Boil and fry eggs until the white
and the yolk are solid. Don't eat uncooked food made from raw eggs – for example home-made mayon-
naise or ice-cream. Avoid drinks with ice cubes. Symptoms are severe stomach pains, diarrhoea, vomiting, and fever. Young people recover after one to three days in bed, but older and weaker people sometimes have to be taken to hospital. They may even die.

7. _____ is caused by a virus and affects the liver. To avoid catching it, you have to
disinfect your hands very carefully before and after assisting. You should disinfect and sterilize instruments by steam under pressure. Be careful with blood. Always wear rubber gloves. You should be vaccinated against this occupational disease.

Please work in groups and translate one of the following:
1. texts 1, 2, 7   **2.** text 3   **3.** texts 4, 5   **4.** text 6

Write about your own experience with infectious diseases. Write about 60 words.

Let's talk about AIDS (Acquired Immune Deficiency Syndrome)
When the immune system is out of order, people cannot fight against infections. This is what happens with
people who have AIDS. They die of infections like pneumonia. AIDS was first reported in the United States
in 1981. It is caused by a virus (HIV) spread by sexual contact, needle sharing or exchange of blood (transfusions). People at highest risk for HIV infection include homosexual and bisexual men, intravenous drug
users, and hemophiliacs. Others with high risks are prostitutes, people who received blood transfusions,
and babies who were born by mothers infected with HIV. You can get it by having sex with a member of a
high-risk group without using condoms. You can't get it by shaking hands or sharing drinks with a person
who has AIDS. You can't get it in swimming-pools or on toilet seats. You can even kiss an infected person
on the lips.
AIDS has already killed more Americans than the Vietnam War – more than 72,000 until 1990. Everything
must be done to prevent this disease, because almost everyone who catches it will die of it.

Please translate:

1. kämpfen gegen _____

2. Lungenentzündung _____

3. übertragen durch _____

4. Fixer _____

5. Bluter _____

6. Bluttransfusionen erhalten _____

Please fill in the table.

How can you get AIDS?	How can't you get AIDS?

"He lied to me and now I'm HIV-positive"

HIV wasn't an issue for me. My fault was to love a man who was bisexual. Peter never told me that he met boys for love. I was so sure. We never used condoms. – Never have unprotected sex! ! ! For me, this advice was too late. I never knew that the man I lived with was HIV-positive.

The man I trusted completely infected me with the virus. He was 25, a musician, good-looking, funny and
5 intelligent. I didn't know he had sex with other men. To me he didn't look like someone who had AIDS. He didn't have swollen lymph nodes, a rash, weight loss, or fever. I couldn't believe that Peter could have it. I went for a test and it was positive. I asked Peter why he'd never told me, but he said he couldn't bear the thought of losing me.

Most of my friends, my family and colleagues have been wonderful. Peter died just before Christmas. On
10 the one hand, I hated him, but on the other hand, I felt sad for him. I have a real problem trusting men now. I'm not ashamed of being HIV-positive anymore. I can have sex when I take precautions – condoms and spermicidal cream. HIV is constantly destroying my white blood cells, called the Helper T-cells, my body's defence against infections. I have been treated with a combination of medicines to fight HIV infection. This is called antiretroviral therapy (ART). It can control the virus so that I might live a longer and happier life. It
15 even can reduce the risk of transmitting HIV to others.

Please find the correct expressions from the text above.

1. not to tell the truth _____

2. an important problem _____

3. a mistake _____

4. giving help and information _____

5. to believe that someone is honest _____

6. red spots on the skin _____

7. an action which prevents something dangerous from happening _____

8. damaging _____

9. action which protects a person from attack by microorganisms _____

Please discuss your way of dealing with AIDS with your classmates.

1. Are **you** worried about getting AIDS?
2. How do **you** protect yourself against AIDS in the surgery?
3. How do **you** protect yourself in your private life?

This advertisement was published in a youth magazine:

HOW FAR WILL YOU GO BEFORE YOU MENTION CONDOMS?

THIS FAR?

THIS FAR?

Today, no one can ignore the need to mention condoms. Have sex with someone without using one and not only could you risk an unwanted pregnancy, but you also risk contracting one of the many sexually transmitted diseases.

Like Herpes, Chlamydia, Gonorrhoea, and of course HIV, the virus which leads to AIDS.

When is the easiest moment to say you want to use one? How about while you're still wearing your knickers.

By now you've gone far enough to make it obvious that you both want to have sex. But not so far that you're in danger of getting emotionally and sexually carried away.

So the question isn't if, but when you mention condoms. You could mention them at any moment leading up to sexual intercourse. In reality, it's not quite so easy.

Mention them too early and you might feel you look pushy or available. Leave it too late and you risk getting so carried away you might not mention them at all.

It's a perfect opportunity. So take it. Say you want to use a condom.

Say he hasn't got one? Well, have one of your own at the ready just in case. It really doesn't matter whose you use. And then you can go just as far as you like.

Source: Cray, Stern, Biocca, Communicating about Risks to Environment and Health in Europe,
Springer US: 2013

Please translate the text and comment on the pictures.
Heute kann niemand mehr die Notwendigkeit, Kondome zu erwähnen, ignorieren …

Please work in small groups and create an advertisement which motivates young people like you to protect themselves against AIDS.

Let's talk about HPV (Human Papilloma Virus)

During the last seven years there has been a continual rise in cervical cancer caused by viruses. Genital human papillomavirus (HPV) is the most common sexually transmitted infection. Most people who become infected with HPV do not even know they have it and pass the virus to a sex partner. Because of this virus you can get cervical cancer. You will experience no symptoms.

If you are lucky your gynaecologist tells you to get screened. The PAP test is a cervical cancer screening and can identify abnormal or pre-cancerous changes in the cervix so that they can be removed before cancer develops.

A vaccine can protect female patients from HPV. It is recommended for 11 to 12 year old girls. Ideally you should get the vaccine before your first sexual contact. Condoms may lower the risk of HPV, if used all the time. And how do you really know if you are in a mutually faithful relationship with somebody who has had no other sex partners.

Pair-work:
Work with a student and develop ideas, how young girls can prevent HPV.

What you should do if a friend of yours is suffering from cancer:

- Be a good listener. Listen to what is said and how it is said.
- Endure silence. It may help the friend to concentrate on his/her thoughts and emotions. If you are constantly talking, the person can be irritated and suffer from your nervousness.
- Maintain eye contact. Touching, smiling and looks that show affection prove the friend that you care for her/him as you always have.
- Do not give advice.
- Do not be overprotective.
- Do not say "I know how you feel".
- If you have to cry, do it. Don't pretend to be strong if you are not.
- Share activities with the person outside and inside of the house.
- Do not avoid contact. Visit and call the friend as often as you can.
- Ask the person for help and support if you need it.
- Be yourself - let your words and actions come from your heart.

Group-work:
Work in small groups of four students. Discuss the list and add things you find important.

6.7 The dangers of smoking, alcoholism and drug abuse

Daniela: Rebekka, can't you put out that terrible cigarette? Don't you know that smoke is bad for your baby?

Rebekka: *Oh, Danni, why can't you allow me just nine or ten cigarettes a day during pregnancy?*

Daniela: It would be better if you stopped smoking.

Rebekka: *I've tried to do it, but I seem to need the nicotine. It calms my nerves and I feel better after a day in the surgery. Cigarettes help me to fight stress. In the morning, they are good for concentration.*

Daniela: Nonsense! Sometimes you really smell when you assist. The smoke sticks to your hair, your white coat and your breath. As a dental assistant you shouldn't smell. Patients may think they have an ashtray in front of their faces. Besides, every cigarette is poison for your baby. All that dirt goes down into your body. Do you want your baby to be underweight and in poor health? You make him or her a passive smoker. If you were intelligent and responsible you wouldn't smoke.

Rebekka: *Nonsense! I don't think smoking is as dangerous as doctors tell you. All this stuff about lung cancer and heart disease doesn't prevent people from smoking. And I've cut down a lot lately to protect my baby. I used to smoke two packets a day.*

Daniela: I think it's a bad and smelly habit, which can seriously damage your and your baby's health.

Please explain the following words in English.

1. pregnancy _____

2. ashtray _____

3. poison _____

4. passive smoker _____

5. responsible _____

Please list Daniela's and Rebekka's arguments.

Daniela's arguments against smoking	Rebekka's arguments for smoking
_____	_____
_____	_____
_____	_____
_____	_____
_____	_____
_____	_____
_____	_____

Please form small groups. One of each group should interview the others.
Please note the outcome of the interviews.

1. Is there anyone here who smokes?

1. _____

2. Who of you smokes the most cigarettes?

2. _____

3. How much money do you spend on cigarettes?

3. _____

4. Should a dental assistant be allowed to smoke in the surgery? Give reasons.

4. _____

5. Why do you smoke? Give reasons.

5. _____

6. Has anybody of you ever tried to stop smoking?

6. _____

7. What are the negative effects of smoking?

7. _____

I'm an alcoholic

My name is Silke. I have been an alcoholic for two years now. Everything started when my husband Peter left me and our little daughter Mirja. He had found a more attractive woman he wanted to live with.

In the privacy of my home, I began my career as an alcoholic. Nobody noticed it. I could easily buy my bottles in big supermarkets. My family and friends understood that I wanted to spend the evenings together
5 with Mirja. While my daughter was sleeping, I secretly drank one glass of wine after the other. Wine could not solve my problems. I became dependent on it. Body and mind needed more and more of the drug to have the same effect.

I took the risk of ruining my life. The problems were getting worse and worse. At work, I was usually moody, aggressive and tired. I used to come too late or even to stay at home when I felt miserable in the morning. My
10 boss fired me when he found a bottle of wine in my desk. I was out of work and was totally ashamed of myself.

Some months later I lost my best friends. They couldn't understand why I stole money from my sister to buy alcohol. I didn't care about it.

By drinking more and more, I could forget Peter and his new love. I felt free and flew high. Then came the horror and the nightmares, the pain and the tears. Mirja was taken away from me. Will alcohol destroy my
15 life completely?

Please translate the text into German. You may use a dictionary.

Ich bin Alkoholikerin
Ich heiße Silke …

Comprehension – Please answer in complete sentences.

1. What was the trigger (Auslöser) that caused Silke's alcoholism?
2. Where did she start drinking?
3. What did Silke drink and where did she buy her bottles?
4. Did anybody notice her addiction?
5. When did she usually drink alcohol?
6. Why didn't she stop drinking?
7. Why did she lose her job?
8. Why was Silke ashamed of herself?
9. How did she lose her friends?
10. How did Silke feel when she drank alcohol?

What will happen to Silke? Think up a possible end. Write about 60–80 words.

What do you know about drugs?
Please complete the text with the following words. Some words may have to be used more than once.

cocaine – sedatives – heroin – stimulants – crack – methadone

1. _____ is a pain killer and a narcotic. The drug is injected directly into the blood. It reaches the brain fast and takes effect quickly. By sharing a needle, the addict can get or pass on the

   HIV to other addicts. An overdose of _____ can lead to death.

2. _____ , sometimes called "coke", is a stimulant, which makes people feel wonderful and energetic. People inhale it and get "high" and may have hallucinations. This means that they see things which aren't there. They also have strange feelings.

3. _____ is cocaine sold in little pieces. Those pieces are put in a pipe and are

   then smoked. _____ ruins lives. It is cheaper than cocaine and easier to get. The drug needs only eight seconds to reach the brain.

4. _____ speed up the brain and nerves so that people do not feel tired.

5. _____ such as sleeping pills make people feel sleepy.

6. Drugs must be withdrawn from the addict's body. It is a difficult and painful process. The addict is sick

   and trembles. Instead of going "cold-turkey" the addict can take _____. It is a substitute drug, which takes away the craving for heroin.

Please explain the following expressions in English.

1. to share a needle _____

2. an overdose _____

3. to withdraw _____

4. cold-turkey _____

5. substitute drug _____

6. craving _____

Grammar Revision

The Passive

This is a typical **active** sentence:
Robert Koch discovered the tubercle bacterium.

"The tubercle bacterium" ist das Objekt dieses Aktivsatzes. Es wird im Passivsatz zum Subjekt und wird an den Satzanfang gestellt.
Das Subjekt des Aktivsatzes "Robert Koch" wird im Passivsatz zum Objekt und mit Hilfe von "by" angefügt.

Transformed into the **passive**, this sentence looks like the following:
The tubercle bacterium was discovered by Robert Koch.

Das Passiv wird gebildet aus einer Form von **to be** and **past participle**:

Ich werde behandelt:	I am treated
Ich wurde behandelt:	I was treated
Ich bin behandelt worden:	I have been treated
Ich war behandelt worden:	I had been treated
Ich werde behandelt werden:	I will be treated
Ich werde behandelt worden sein:	I will have been treated
Ich würde behandelt:	I would be treated
Ich würde behandelt worden sein:	I would have been treated

Please translate:

1. Ich wurde gestern geimpft.

_____

2. Viele Menschen wurden durch Impfstoffe geschützt.

_____

3. Lebensmittelvergiftung wird durch Salmonellen verursacht.

_____

4. Meine Tochter wurde mir weggenommen.

_____

5. Umweltverschmutzung kann durch Wiederverwertung vermieden werden.

_____

Please transform the following sentences into the passive.

1. We showed the patient the results of his examination.

   _____

2. Sandy wrote a letter.

   _____

3. The doctor should have told her the truth.

   _____

4. Susan has not read the medical articles yet.

   _____

5. Miriam painted a picture for our boss.

   _____

6. He offered me a cup of tea.

   _____

7. Dr Augustine examined me.

   _____

8. Sandra invited Susan to the party.

   _____

9. My parents gave up smoking.

   _____

10. Simone ate a hamburger.

   _____

Please create four passive sentences regarding your work.

1. _____

2. _____

3. _____

4. _____

Would you like to work in an English-speaking country?

7.1 Job advertisements

DON'T WORRY – BE HAPPY!!!

Dr Hall and we are looking forward to having you in our dental team if you:

- really work with a smile on your face;
- love crazy patients and a hectic atmosphere;
- enjoy having fun with colleagues;
- don't always think about holidays, a rise in salary and avoiding overtime.

Join us! We are waiting for your application.

Write full details to:
Team Dr Robert Hall, 751 Markham Road, Scarborough/Toronto.

THIS IS THE KEY TO YOUR SUCCESS

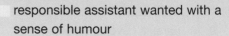

Why not thinking about a career with excellent prospects – even as a doctor's assistant?

- responsible assistant wanted with a sense of humour
- pleasant working conditions
- four-day week
- acceptable salary
- additional payment for overtime
- six weeks holidays per year

You'll be on your feet most of the day, so you should be physically fit.

For further information please ring
Dr Mulroony 438-9388

Please explain the following words in English.

1. job advertisement _____

2. holidays _____

3. a rise in salary _____

4. to avoid overtime _____

5. application _____

6. success _____

7. career _____

8. responsible _____

Please study the two advertisements offering a vacancy in Toronto.

1. What are the differences between the two advertisements?
2. Describe the kind of person the team of Dr Hall is looking for.
3. Dr Mulroony offers pleasant working conditions. Give at least four examples of pleasant working conditions you would like to have in your job.
4. Would you apply for any of these vacancies? Give reasons for your decision.

Please discuss in the class.

Imagine your boss wants to employ a new assistant/PKA. He asks you to decide who of the applicants will get the job. The following is a list of qualities the applicants wrote they had. Which five of these qualities do you consider most important for your job? Give reasons for your choice and discuss them in class.

patient	helpful
calm	pretty
reliable	cheerful
discreet	sympathetic towards patients
careful	cooperative
friendly	able to explain clearly
healthy	able to understand children and elderly patients
intelligent	

Make a list of negative qualities which you in your job shouldn't have.

_____

_____

_____

_____

_____

_____

_____

_____

_____

_____

_____

Tell the class about your job. Write about 100 words.

You can use the following terms:

I like	I don't like
I quite like	I dislike
I am fond of	I hate
I love	I can't stand
I am content with	I am not satisfied with
I am not keen on	

Dagmar Lies
Merianweg 22

30655 Hannover
Germany   20. April, ...

Dr Hall
751 Markham Road
Scarborough
Toronto
Canada

Dear Dr Hall,

My sister Silvia lives with her family in Toronto. She was impressed by the funny advertisement she saw in the newspaper. I would like to join your team and so I want to apply for the vacancy of a dental assistant in your surgery.

My curriculum vitae with details about my qualifications is enclosed. I have been working as a dental assistant for five years.

I enjoy working with people. At the moment, I'm responsible for instructing our apprentices. I am accustomed to working hard in our surgery. Working overtime is no problem for me.

I am particularly interested in Canadian history and literature. My hobbies are travelling and reading.

I would like to work in your surgery because I want to improve my English and to get to know Canadian dentistry. My knowledge of English is fairly good because I stayed with my sister's family in Toronto for a year after my Abitur.

Although I enjoy my present job, I hope you will give me the opportunity of an interview. In two weeks time I will be in Toronto for my holidays. Please phone my sister in Toronto. Her number is 585-2377.

Yours sincerely

Dagmar Lies

Enclosures
curriculum vitae
references

Dagmar's colleagues in Germany want to know what Dagmar wrote to Dr Hall. Please translate the letter for them.

Sehr geehrter Dr. Hall,
meine Schwester Silvia wohnt …

7.3 Curriculum Vitae

CURRICULUM VITAE

Name:	Dagmar Lies
Address:	Merianweg 22
	30655 Hanover
	Germany
Telephone:	0511/12345
	Silvia Montgomery
	Toronto 585-2377
	(sister)
Date of birth:	9 May, 1993
Place of birth:	Osnabrück
Marital status:	Single, no children
Nationality:	German

Education:	2003-2011	Gymnasium Hannover
	2011-2012	Various jobs in Toronto (Burger King, Best Western)
	2012-2014	Vocational training as a dental assistant at Dr Roman Knauer's surgery, Hannover
Work experience:	2014-2016	Surgery Dr Wagner, Hannover
	Present salary:	1620 euro(s)
	Special skills:	X-ray certificate, preventive-dental-care-certificate

Study Dagmar's curriculum vitae. Write your personal curriculum vitae, using Dagmar's as a model.

Look at the information and ask questions for the underlined parts.

1. I live in Hannover. _____ *Where do you live?* _____

2. I was born in 1993. _____

3. My sister Silvia lives in Toronto with her family. _____

4. I am single and have no children. _____

5. My present salary is 1 620 euro(s). _____

6. I have got an X-ray certificate and a preventive-dental-care-certificate.

_____

7. Dagmar is applying for a job in Dr Hall's surgery because she wants to improve her English.

_____

7.4 The interview

Dagmar is invited for an interview with Dr Hall and his team.

Please work in groups of four. Write a dialogue and play the roles of Dr Hall, Dagmar, assistant Diana and assistant Sandra.

Dr Hall welcomes Dagmar and introduces himself and his team. He tells her that it's nice to meet her and asks her to take a seat.

Dagmar thanks Dr Hall and introduces herself.

Diana wants to know how old Dagmar is and whether she has got a boy friend in Germany.

Dagmar tells her that she is single at the moment and wants to leave Germany for two or three years.

Sandra asks Dagmar why she would like to work in Canada.

Dagmar tells her that she visited Toronto several times. She says that she loves hiking, canoeing and wilderness camping.

Diana wants to know what Dagmar's skills and qualifications are.

Dagmar tells her about the training in Germany and about the two courses she took at the Zahnärztekammer. Dagmar asks Dr Hall how much money she would earn.

Dr Hall tells her that she would get 320 Canadian dollars a week.

Dagmar says that she would be satisfied with the pay, that she could live with her sister's family and would not need to rent a flat. She asks how many hours she would have to work.

Dr Hall tells her that she would have to work eight hours a day. He mentions that he requires some overtime occasionally.

Dagmar tells him that that's no problem for her.

Dr Hall tells Dagmar he will employ her. He asks her whether she can begin in August.

Dagmar is happy. She asks the team what her tasks will be and how the others spend their free time.

Sandra tells her that she will assist in the treatment room and will take and develop X-rays. She offers Dagmar to join Diana and her when they play tennis or go to the disco.

Dagmar will be working in Canada where she will be able to improve her English.

Can you think of other English-speaking countries where you could work or which you would like to visit?

Please give examples:

1. _____   4. _____

2. _____   5. _____

3. _____   6. _____

Before thinking of going abroad for a job or on holidays you should get some information on the country.

You could write to the following institutions:

Zentralstelle für Arbeitsvermittlung
Ville Mombler Str. 76
53123 Bonn

Britische Botschaft
Wilhelmstr. 70–71
10117 Berlin

Kanadische Botschaft
Friedrichstr. 95
10117 Berlin

Botschaft der Vereinigten Staaten von Amerika
Neustädtische Kirchstr. 4–5
10117 Berlin

Australische Botschaft
Friedrichstr. 200
10117 Berlin

In the next sections you will get an idea what to expect in Great Britain and the United States of America.

7.5 The National Health Service in Great Britain

In Great Britain, there's a public health service under government administration which covers the whole population – and it is free, except minor charges (Gebühren)! The NHS, which is financed through taxes, gives free basic medical and hospital treatment to
5 every British citizen and even to visitors from the European Community. This system has got increasing financial problems because the growth of medical technology has made health care (especially hospital care) more expensive.

Help is provided at three different levels: **general practitioner**
10 **(family doctor) and dental services, hospital and specialist services, and local health authority services.**

The first contact with the National Health Service is usually through the general practitioner (GP), who is sometimes called the family doctor. But different to Germany, GPs work together in small
15 teams in Britain and form practices, which cover a certain neighbourhood or part of a town. The consultations of the GP are free and every citizen must be registered with a GP in the UK. Every citizen gets a NHS-number when registered for the first time which he keeps all his life.
20 But the GPs are only one part of the National Health Service who deal with people's every day health problems, often called "primary care". Along with the GPs there are lots of health professionals like nurses, dentists, health visitors, pharmacists and a wide range of therapists who work alongside with the family doctors. Sometimes
25 you find them in the same building, sometimes in own practices

Big Ben, London, Großbritannien

somewhere in town. The service they provide together is an important part of prevention and health care - and treating people who are ill.

In general, all services offered by GP practices are free to patients, although there sometimes might be a small charge for prescriptions. People with a low income, elderly people and children are absolutely free of charge. All the health specialists working in primary care also have a wider role in supporting the health needs of
30 the local people. They work together with health authorities and set up plans, how the best service can be provided. And this role will be even more important within the next years, as primary health care should take over more responsibility for helping to shape the pattern of local health services.

Doctors in the UK may also have private patients, like in Germany, who pay for their treatment individually. The responsibilities of primary care through GPs, nurses, dentists and pharmacists are big these days.
35 Screening, immunisation, vaccination, contraceptive advice, health education and access to information are gaining more and more importance to the health care of the people. After assessment and diagnosis of the GP help is often needed from specialists, who are linked via modern technical equipment.

Professionals and doctors working for the hospital and specialist services get government salaries as these institutions are government-owned and are under the direction of so-called hospital boards. As in
40 Germany, getting the patients back into their normal environment as fast as possible is preferred as soon as hospital treatment is no longer needed.

Maternity and child welfare, post hospital care, home nursing and various preventing services are provided by local health authority services. You will also find institutions for family planning and day nurseries there. It goes without saying that there are of course services for older people, emergency care services and
45 services for people with special needs.

For further information on the British health system visit www.nhs.uk

Please give the German expressions:

1. increasing _____

2. vaccination _____

3. primary care team _____

4. maternity _____

5. family-planning _____

Compare the German health system with the new NHS by finding out similarities and differences. Make up a table!

7.6 How do Americans pay their medical bills ?

Who doesn't know American TV series like "Emergency Room" etc.? Lots of friendly nurses and qualified doctors help patients in no time, often working for many hours without getting any sleep, but a smile and a handshake after a successful operation from the patients wherever they come from. Is this reality in the United States?

5 There is no social health system like in Germany, so people pay for private health insurances - if they are rich enough! Those who can't afford a private health insurance are covered by two social programmes that provide help for more than 75 million Americans: MEDICARE and MEDICAID.

MEDICARE is the nation's largest health insurance programme, which covers
10 approx. 50 million Americans who are over 65 years of age and those who have permanent kidney failure or certain disabilities. This program contains two parts: Part A, the hospital insurance, and Part B, the medical insurance. (Since 1997 there's been a part C: Medicare+Choice program, a supplement for private insurance) The costs for Medicare total more than $ 450 billion a year! But see in the chart
15 below what Americans have to pay these days:

Freiheitsstatue, New York, USA

Medicare Part B (Medical Insurance):	What you pay in 2016:
Medical and other services. Doctor's services, outpatient medical and surgical services and supplies, diagnostic tests, ambulatory surgery, durable medical equipment, such as wheelchairs, hospital beds, etc. Also physical and occupational therapy, including speech-language therapy and mental health service.	You pay: – $ 166 once per calendar year – 20 % of the approved amount – 20 % for all outpatient therapy services – 40 % (20% from 2017) for most outpatient mental health
Clinical Laboratory Service: Blood tests, urinanalysis, and more	You pay: – Nothing for the services
Home Health Care: Part-time skilled care, home health aide service, durable medical equipment and other supplies	You pay: – Nothing for the services – 20 % of approved amount for durable equip.
Dental Services Medicare doesn't cover routine dental care or most dental procedures such as cleanings, fillings, tooth extractions, or dentures. Medicare doesn't pay for dental plates or other dental devices.	You pay: – 100%
Custodial Care Medicare doesn't cover custodial care when it's the only kind of care you need. Care is considered custodial when it's for the purpose of helping you with activities of daily living or personal needs that could be done safely and reasonably by people without professional skills or training. For example, custodial care includes help getting in and out of bed, bathing, dressing, eating, and taking medicine.	You pay: – 100%

MEDICAID is now a jointly funded, state health insurance programme for certain low-income and needy people. It covers ap. 35 million individuals including children, the aged, blind, and/or disabled, and people who are eligible to receive social security.

But millions of Americans are not covered by any of the programmes, either because they are not poor enough to get MEDICAID, or because the insurance companies don't insure them as they for example are infected with HIV and are likely to get AIDS. Especially people, who don't have a regular income, often Blacks and Hispanics or single-parent families with a low income, tend to be without any medical coverage more often than white, middle-aged Americans and married couples. And even these days you may not be admitted to some hospitals if you cannot prove that you have the money to pay for an operation...

Comprehension and comment – Please answer the questions in as much detail as possible.

1. What picture do we get of American doctors and nurses from TV?
2. Who qualifies for the MEDICARE programme?
3. Do patients have to pay for that programme? Give examples!
4. Who benefits of the MEDICAID programme?
5. Why do a lot of Americans have no health insurance at all?
6. Which groups of American society tend to be without medical coverage? Can you imagine why?
7. Do you think medical treatment should generally be absolutely free for everyone? Give reasons for your opinion by weighing up pros and cons.

For further information on the American health system visit **www.medicare.gov**

7.7 Internet Research

Make an Internet Research and find information about the health systems in Great Britain and the United States.

Work in small groups of four to six students. Produce a poster and present your product to the class. Exhibit the posters at your vocational school.
Use the Internet links and addresses that are given in the chapters before as well as the following ones:

Use **www.google.de**
Go to "The National Health Service".

Use **www.google.de**
Go to "MEDICAID" and "MEDICARE".

For some general information visit
Use **www.wikipedia.com**

Vocabulary English-German

A

ap.	ungefähr
abuse	Missbrauch
access	Zugang
accident	Unfall
according to	bezüglich, betreffend
accusatory	anklagend, beschuldigend
(to) ache	schmerzen, Schmerzen
acid	Säure
action	Handlung
actor	Schauspieler
to add	hinzufügen, addieren
addict	Süchtiger, Abhängiger
administration	Verwaltung
admittance	Zutritt
adult	Erwachsener
advantage	Vorteil
advice	Empfehlung, Ratschlag
to advise	raten, empfehlen
to affect	beeinflussen
affection	Zuneigung
to afford	sich leisten
age	Alter
agitation	Aufregung
to aggravate	verschlimmern
agreement	Abkommen
air pollution	Luftverschmutzung
allergy	Allergie
aloofness	Reserviertheit
although	obwohl
amount	Betrag
to anaesthetize	betäuben
anger	Zorn, Wut
angle	Winkel
animal	Tier
anorexia nervosa	Magersucht
antibody	Antikörper
antiretroviral therapy	antiretrovirale Therapie
anxiety	Angst
anxious	besorgt, beunruhigt
to appear	erscheinen
appendix	Wurmfortsatz
application	Anwendung, Bewerbung
to apply	anwenden
to apply for	sich bewerben um
appointment	Termin
approved	anerkannt, gebilligt
apprentice	Lehrling, Auszubildender
approximate	annähernd, ungefähr
artery	Arterie
ashtray	Aschenbecher
assessment	Beurteilung, Bewertung
to assist	assistieren
to associate	verbinden, assoziieren
attack	Angriff
to attend	(Schule) besuchen
attention	Aufmerksamkeit
attitude	Haltung, Einstellung
available	verfügbar
average	Durchschnitt
to avoid	vermeiden
awful	schrecklich

B

back	Rücken
bacterium	Bakterium
bandage	Verband
bandage scissors	Verbandschere
basic instruments	Grundinstrumente
bat	Fledermaus
to bear	ertragen
bedclothes	Bettzeug
bed jacket	Bettjäckchen
bedside table	Nachtschränkchen
behaviour	Verhalten
to belong to	gehören zu
benefit	Nutzen
best-before date	Verfallsdatum
beyond	jenseits, über...hinaus
bile	Gallensaft
bill	Rechnung
bin	Abfallbehälter
biting surface	Kaufläche
bladder	Blase
blank	Lücke
blanket	Decke
bleaching	Bleichen von Zähnen
blood	Blut
blood picture	Blutbild
blood pressure	Blutdruck
blood sugar test	Blutzuckertest
blood vessel	Blutgefäß
to be blue	deprimiert sein
body	Körper
body language	Körpersprache
bone	Knochen
booster injection	Auffrischungsimpfung
to bother	plagen, quälen
bra	Büstenhalter
brace	Klammer
brain	Gehirn
brain cells	Gehirnzellen
brave	tapfer
break	Pause
breast	Brust
breath	Atem
to breathe	atmen
breathing	Atmung
breed	Zucht, Rasse, Art
bridge	Brücke
to bring up	aufziehen, erziehen
bristle	Borste
brooch	Brosche
to brush one`s teeth	sich die Zähne putzen

C

cake of soap	Stück Seife
calculation	Berechnung
camomile	Kamille
cancer	Krebs
canine	Eckzahn, Caninus
carbohydrates	Kohlenhydrate
cardiologist	Kardiologe (Herzspezialist)
to care for	sorgen für, sich kümmern um

careful	sorgfältig	cough sweets	Hustenbonbons
caries	Karies	cough syrup	Hustensirup
carrots	Möhren	cough tea	Hustentee
cartilage	Knorpel	counter	Handverkaufstisch
cauliflower	Blumenkohl	to cover	bedecken, abdecken
to cause	verursachen, Ursache	coverage	Versicherungsschutz
cavity	Kavität, Loch im Zahn	craving for	Verlangen nach
cell	Zelle	crown	Krone
cement	Zement	cucumber	Gurke
certificate	Zeugnis, Bescheinigung	curable	heilbar
cervics	Gebärmutterhals	(to) cure	heilen, Heilung
chain	Kette	curriculum vitae	Lebenslauf
challenging	herausfordernd, schwierig	custodial	pflegerisch
change	Veränderung	customer	Kunde
(to) charge	Gebühr, belasten	cut	schneiden
chart	Tabelle	cytotoxic drugs	Zytostatika
to chat	plaudern, sich unterhalten		
to check	überprüfen	**D**	
check-up	gründliche Untersuchung		
cheek	Wange	to damage	schaden, beschädigen
cheerful	heiter, fröhlich	damaged	beschädigt
chemist	Apotheker	damp	feucht
cervical cancer	Gebärmutterhalskrebs	dangerous	gefährlich
chest	Brust	day nursery	Kinderhort, Kinderkrippe
choice	Auswahl, Wahl	death	Tod
to choose	auswählen	death sentence	Todesurteil
circular	kreisförmig	decay	Zahnfäule
circulatory system	Kreislaufsystem	to decide	entscheiden
citizen	Bürger, Bürgerin	decision	Entscheidung
classmates	Klassenkameraden	defence	Verteidigung
clot	Blutgerinnsel	to defend against	verteidigen gegen
collar bone	Schlüsselbein	delivery	Warensendung
cold	Erkältung	demand	Nachfrage
cold-turkey	totale Entziehung	dementia	Demenz
colleague	Kollege	dental chair	zahnärztlicher
to collect	sammeln, einsammeln		Behandlungsstuhl
coltsfood	Huflattich	dental assistant	Zahnmedizinische
column	Spalte		Fachangestellte
comb	Kamm	dental dictionary	Zahnmedizinisches
comfortable	bequem		Wörterbuch
to comment on	seine Meinung äußern über	dental floss	Zahnseide
common	gewöhnlich	dental plate	Zahnprothese
companion	Gefährte	dental sealants	Versiegeler
to compare	vergleichen	dental surgery	Zahnarztpraxis
complain	sich beschweren	dental technician	Zahntechniker
to complete	vervollständigen	dentine	Zahnbein
composite filling	Kunststoff-Füllung	dentist	Zahnarzt
computerized	im Rechner gespeicherte	to depend on	abhängen von
records	Karteikarten	dependent on	abhängig von
concerning	betreffend, bezüglich	deprivation	Entzug
to conduct	ausführen, durchführen	dermatologist	Hautarzt
confused	verwirrt	to describe	beschreiben
to connect	verbinden	to destroy	zerstören
conscious	bewußt	destructive	zerstörerisch
to consist of	bestehen aus	to develop	entwickeln
constipation	Verstopfung	to devise	entwickeln, sich
consulting hours	Sprechstundenzeiten		ausdenken
consulting room	Sprechzimmer	diabetes	Zuckerkrankheit
contact lenses	Kontaktlinsen	diabetic	Diabetiker
to contain	beinhalten, enthalten	dialogue	Dialog
contaminated	verseucht	diarrhoea	Durchfall
contents	Inhalt	to die	sterben
contraceptive advice	Beratung über	diet	Diät, Ernährung
	Verhütungsmittel	to differ from	sich unterscheiden von
contradictory	widersprüchlich	to digest	verdauen
conversation	Unterhaltung	digestion	Verdauung
to convince	überzeugen	digestive system	Verdauungssystem
to cope with	gewachsen sein	to dilute	abschwächen
coronary artery	Herzkranzgefäß	dining-room	Essraum
cotton bud	Wattestäbchen	disabled	behindert
to cough	husten	to disappear	verschwinden
cough drops	Hustentropfen	discovery	Entdeckung

disease	Krankheit
dish	Gericht, Speise
disinfection	Desinfektion
to display	auslegen
disposable	wegwerfbar
dissatisfied	unzufrieden
to distract oneself	sich ablenken
to distribute	verteilen
divorce	Scheidung
dizzy	schwindelig
doctor	Arzt
doctor's assistant	Medizinische Fachangestellte
documentation	Dokumentation
to draw	zeichnen, ziehen
drawer	Schublade
drug	Medikament, Droge
drug allergy	Arzneimittelallergie
durable equipment	Dauerleihgabe
during	während
dust	Staub

E

e.g.	zum Beispiel
ear	Ohr
early detection	Früherkennung
earnings	Verdienstmöglichkeiten
earpiece	Ohrstück
to ease	lindern, erleichtern
elbow	Ellenbogen
elder care center	Pflegeheim für ältere Personen
eligible	berechtigt
to eliminate	entfernen
embarrassed	verlegen
emergency	Notfall
emotions	Gefühle
emphasis	Betonung
to employ	einstellen, beschäftigen
employees	Beschäftigte
employer	Arbeitgeber
employment	Beschäftigung, Arbeit
enamel	Zahnschmelz
endocrine system	Hormonsystem
endodontics	Wurzelkanalbehandlung
endoscope	Endoskop
to endure	ertragen
to enhance	erhöhen, vergrößern
to enjoy	genießen
ENT specialist	Hals-Nasen-Ohren-Arzt
environment	Umfeld, Umgebung, Umwelt
equivalent	Entsprechung
especially	insbesondere
estrogen	Östrogen
examination	Untersuchung, Prüfung
examination couch	Untersuchungsliege
to examine	untersuchen
except	außer
exciting	aufregend
exemption	Ausnahme
exhausted	erschöpft
to exhibit	ausstellen
to expect	erwarten
(to) experience	Erfahrung, erfahren
to explain	begründen, erklären
expression	Ausdruck
extraction forceps	Extraktionszange
eye	Auge
to evolve	entfalten

F

facility	Einrichtung
to failure	versagen
fair skin	helle Haut
faithful	treu
fallopian tube	Eileiter
false	falsch
fault	Fehler
fear	Furcht
fee	Gebühr
to feed	füttern
female	weiblich
fennel	Fenchel
ferret	Frettchen
fever	Fieber
feverish	fiebrig
file card	Karteikarte
file card box	Karteikasten
to fill in	ausfüllen
filling materials	Füllungsmaterialien
firm	fest
flat charge	Pauschale
flu	Grippe
food	Lebensmittel
food allergy	Lebensmittelallergie
food poisoning	Lebensmittelvergiftung
to force	zwingen
forehead	Stirn
forename	Vorname
frequently	häufig
frequency	Frequenz
frightened	ängstlich
front tooth	Frontzahn
functions	Funktionen
fungus	Pilz
furrowed	zusammengezogen

G

gall bladder	Gallenblase
gap	Lücke
gastric flu	Magen-Darm-Grippe
gastroenterologist	Gastroenterologe
gauze bandage	Mullbinde
general	allgemein
general practitioner	Allgemeinmediziner
geriatric nurse	Altenpflegerin, Altenpfleger
gestures	Gesten
gift	Geschenk
gingivitis	Zahnfleischentzündung
gland	Drüse
glasses	Brillengläser
government	Regierung
growth	Wachstum
guinea pig	Meerschweinchen
gum	Zahnfleisch
gum disease	Zahnfleischerkrankung
gum margin	Zahnfleischrand
guy	Typ, Kerl
gynaecologist	Frauenarzt

H

haematologist	Hämatologe
handicapped people	Behinderte
to hand instruments	Instrumente anreichen
head	Kopf
headache	Kopfschmerz
to heal	heilen
health	Gesundheit
health insurance	Krankenversicherung

healthy	gesund	joint	Gelenk
to hear	hören	jointly-funded project	Gemeinschaftsprojekt
hearing aids	Hörgeräte	jumper	Pullover
heart	Herz		
heart attack	Herzanfall, Herzinfarkt	**K**	
heartburn	Sodbrennen		
hemophiliac	Bluter	key qualifications	Schlüsselqualifikationen
to hesitate	zögern	kidney	Niere
to hide	verstecken	knee	Knie
high blood pressure drug	Mittel gegen Bluthochdruck	knickers	Schlüpfer
high-risk patient	Risikopatient	knowledge	Wissen
to hike	wandern		
hole	Loch	**L**	
Hold the line!	Bleiben Sie am Apparat!		
home care team	ambulanter Pflegedienst	(to) label	beschriften, Beschriftung
honest	ehrlich	laboratory	Labor
horsetail	Schachtelhalm	lead apron	Bleischürze
hospital	Krankenhaus	leaflet	Prospekt, Flyer
hospital board	Krankenhausbehörde	letter	Buchstabe
huge	gewaltig, riesig	letter of application	Bewerbungsschreiben
human being	Mensch	lettuce	Salat
hurriedly	gehetzt	to lie	lügen
to hurt	schmerzen	like	Vorliebe
hydrogen peroxide	Wasserstoffsuperoxid	likewise	genauso
hypnosis	Hypnose	link	Verweis, Verbindung
		linseed	Leinsamen
		liquid	Flüssigkeit
		liver	Leber
I		local	örtlich
		locker	Spind, Schließfach
illness	Krankheit	loneliness	Einsamkeit
to imagine	sich etwas vorstellen	to lower	verringern
immune system	Immunsystem	lump	Knoten
impacted	eingeklemmt, impaktiert	lunch	Mittagessen
impression	Eindruck	lung	Lunge
impression material	Abdruckmaterial	lymph node	Lymphknoten
to improve	verbessern	lymph vessel	Lymphgefäß
inability	Unfähigkeit		
incisor	Schneidezahn, Incisivus		
to include	beinhalten	**M**	
increase	Anstieg		
independent	unabhängig	magazine	Zeitschrift
individual work	Einzelarbeit	to maintain	erhalten, pflegen
infectious disease	Infektionskrankheit	malignant	bösartig
inflamed	entzündet	to manage	bewältigen
influenza	Grippe	manner	Verhaltensweise
ingredients	Zutaten	marital status	Familienstand
to inject	injizieren	mashed potatoes	Kartoffelbrei
injection	Injektion, Einspritzung	maternity	Mutterschaft
injury	Verletzung	meals on wheels	Essen auf Rädern
inlay	Einlagefüllung	to measure	messen
to instruct	anleiten, unterweisen	medical card	Krankenversicherungskarte,
instruction	Anweisung		Chipkarte
to insure	versichern		
internet research	Internetrecherche	medical dictionary	Medizinisches Wörterbuch
interproximal brush	Zahnzwischenraumbürste	medical encyclopaedia	Anamnese,
intestines	Eingeweide	medical history	Krankheitsvorgeschichte
intravenuous	intravenös	medical history form	Anamnesebogen
to introduce	vorstellen, einführen	medical record	Karteikarte
invader	Eindringling	memory	Erinnerung
to invent	erfinden	to mention	erwähnen
invisible	unsichtbar	message	Botschaft, Nachricht
invoice	Rechnung	microorganism	Kleinstlebewesen
iron	Eisen	microscope	Mikroskop
to irritate	reizen	microwave	Mikrowelle
issue	Problem, Angelegenheit	mind	Geist, Gedächtnis
itchy	juckend	minor	geringfügig
item	Artikel, Gegenstand	minority	Minderheit
		(to) mirror	Spiegel, spiegeln
		misery	Elend
J		moisture	Feuchtigkeit
		molar	Backenzahn, Molar
jail sentence	Gefängnisstrafe	mole	Muttermal, Leberfleck
jaw bone	Kieferknochen	mood	Stimmung
job advertisement	Stellenanzeige		

moody	launisch, mürrisch	paper tissues	Papiertaschentücher
moreover	außerdem	paralysis	Lähmung
morning shift	Frühschicht	parentheses	Klammern
mouth	Mund	particulars	Personalien
mouth rinse	Munddusche	to pass	übertragen
mouthwash	Mundwasser	past	Vergangenheit
muscle	Muskel	pasta	Nudelgericht
muscle pain	Muskelschmerz	patience	Geduld
mutual	gegenseitig	patient	Patient, geduldig
		pattern	Muster
N		payment obligation	Zahlungsverpflichtung
		peace	Frieden
nail scissors	Nagelschere	peas	Erbsen
nap	Schläfchen, Nickerchen	peppermint	Pfefferminze
nausea	Übelkeit, Brechreiz	periodontics	Parodontalbehandlung
neck	Hals	pet	Haustier
necessary	notwendig	pharmacist	Apotheker
to need	benötigen, brauchen	pharmacy	Apotheke
needle	Nadel, Kanüle	(to) phone	anrufen, Telefon
to neglect	vernachlässigen	phone call	Telefongespräch
neither ... nor	weder ... noch	physical	körperlich
nephew	Neffe	physical exertion	körperliche
nerve endings	Nervenendigungen		Anstrengung
nervous system	Nervensystem	physical strength	körperliche Kraft
neurologist	Nervenarzt	physical therapist	Krankengymnast
night-dress	Nachthemd	physician	Arzt
nightmare	Alptraum	piercing	stechend
nose	Nase	place of residence	Wohnort
to notice	bemerken	plaque	Zahnbelag
nourishing cream	Nährcreme	pneumonia	Lungenentzündung
nutrient	Nährstoff	poem	Gedicht
nutrition	Ernährung	poison	Gift
		population	Bevölkerung
O		post	nach
		possibility	Möglichkeit
occasionally	gelegentlich	posture	Körperhaltung
occupational disease	Berufskrankheit	poverty	Armut
occupational therapy	Beschäftigungstherapie	pre-cancerous	Präkanzerös
to occur	sich ereignen	precaution	Vorsichtsmaßnahme
to offer	anbieten	(to) prefer	bevorzugen
office work	Büroarbeit	pregnancy	Schwangerschaft
ointment	Salbe	pregnant	schwanger
old people's home	Altersheim	premium	Versicherungsprämie
open-minded	aufgeschlossen	pre-molar	kleiner Backenzahn,
ophthalmologist	Augenarzt		Prämolar
opportunity	Gelegenheit	to prepare	zubereiten, vorbereiten
optician	Optiker	to prescribe	verschreiben
optometrist	Optiker	prescription	Rezept
to order	bestellen, anordnen	presentation task	Präsentationsaufgabe
orthodontics	Kieferorthopädie	pressure	Druck
orthopaedist	Orthopäde	to prevent	vorbeugen
outpatient treatment	ambulante Behandlung	prevention	Vorbeugung
(service)		previous	vorhergehend
ovary	Eierstock	primary medical care	medizinische
overdose	Überdosis		Erstbehandlung,
over-the-counter medicine	freiverkäufliches Präparat		-versorgung
overhead overprotective	überbeschützend	probe	Sonde
transparency	OHP-Folie	to process	entwickeln
overtime	Überstunden	to progress	voranschreiten
owner	Besitzer	to promise	versprechen
oxygen	Sauerstoff	to promote	fördern, begünstigen
		prospects	Aussichten
P		prostheses	Prothesen
		prosthetics	Prothetik
pace	hier: Geschwindigkeit	to protect from	schützen vor
paediatrician	Kinderarzt	protection	Schutz
pancreas	Bauchspeicheldrüse	to prove	beweisen
pain	Schmerz	to provide	liefern, bieten, zur
painful	schmerzhaft		Verfügung
painkiller	Schmerzmittel		stellen
painless	schmerzlos	psychiatrist	Psychiater
pair-work	Partnerarbeit	psychologist	Psychologe

public health service	öffentlicher Gesundheitsdienst	**S**	
pulp	Zahnmark	sage	Salbei
puppy	junger Hund	salary	Gehalt
to purify	reinigen	saliva	Speichel
purpose	Zweck	to save	retten
purse	Geldbörse	scalpel	Skalpell
pushy	aufdringlich	scarf	Schal
to put somebody through	jemanden durchstellen	scent	Geruch
		scheduling	Terminplanung
Q		scissors	Schere
quarrel	Streit, Auseinandersetzung	screening	Reihenuntersuchung
questionnaire	Fragebogen	to scroll	rollen
		to scrub	schrubben, scheuern
R		search engine	Suchmaschine
rabies	Tollwut	to search for	suchen nach
rabbit	Kaninchen	secretly	heimlich
radiologist	Radiologe	sedative	Beruhigungsmittel
range	Bandbreite, Angebot	to select	auswählen
rash	Ausschlag	self-esteem	Selbstachtung
to receive	erhalten, bekommen	sensitive	empfindlich
receiver	Telefonhörer	serious	ernst, ernsthaft
recently	kürzlich	to serve	dienen, bedienen
reception	Anmeldung	severe	stark
to recommend	empfehlen	to shape	formen
to recover	sich erholen	to share	teilen
rectum	Mastdarm	sheet	Bettlaken
recuperation	Genesung	shelf	Regal
to reduce	vermindern	to shiver	zittern
to refer	überweisen	shoulder	Schulter
reference	Zeugnis, Referenz	shower	Dusche
referral	Überweisung	sick	krank
to refresh	erfrischen	side effect	Nebenwirkung
refrigerator	Kühlschrank	side tooth	Seitenzahn
regardless	ungeachtet	(to) sign	Zeichen, Türschild; unterschreiben
to register	registrieren		
rejection	Ablehnung	similar	ähnlich
relationship	Beziehung	skeleton	Skelett
to relax	entspannen	to sketch	skizzieren
to release	freisetzen	skill	Fertigkeit, Kenntnis
relief	Erleichterung	skin	Haut
to relieve	mildern, erleichtern	skincare	Hautpflege
remedy	Heilmittel	skirt	Rock
to remove	entfernen	skull	Schädel
to repeat	wiederholen	sleeping pill	Schlaftablette
to replace	ersetzen	sleeplessness	Schlaflosigkeit
report	Bericht	sleeves	Ärmel
reptile	Reptil	slim	schlank
resident	Bewohner	smallpox	Pocken
resistant to	widerstandsfähig gegen	to smell	riechen, Geruch
respiratory system	Atmungssystem	to sneeze	niesen
responsible	verantwortungsbewusst	social security	Sozialhilfe
rsponsibility	Verantwortung	society	Gesellschaft
restorative dentistry	Konservierende Zahnheilkunde	soil	Erde
		to solve	lösen
result	Ergebnis	to soothe	beruhigen
retirement	Pensionierung	sore throat	Halsschmerzen
to reveal	enthüllen	sound wave	Schallwelle
rib	Rippe	spectacles	Brille
to ring up	anrufen	to spell	buchstabieren
rise	Anstieg	sphygmomanometer	Blutdruckmeßgerät
rise in salary	Gehaltserhöhung	spine	Wirbelsäule
root	Wurzel	spot	Pickel
root canal	Wurzelkanal	to spread	ausbreiten
rough	rauh	to squeeze	ausdrücken
rounded	abgerundet	staff cloakroom	Personalraum, Personalgarderobe
rubber glove	Gummihandschuh		
rubella	Röteln	to stain	beflecken, fleckig werden
to ruminate	grübeln	to stamp	stempeln
to run errands	Botengänge machen	steam	Dampf
		sterilization	Sterilisation
		stethoscope	Stethoskop

stinging nettle	Brennessel
to stock up on	auffüllen
stomach	Magen
strain	Druck, Belastung
strange	seltsam
to strengthen	kräftigen, stärken
to strip to the waist	den Oberkörper frei machen
stroke	Schlaganfall
substitute	Ersatz
success	Erfolg
successful	erfolgreich
to suffer from	leiden unter
to suggest	vorschlagen
sunburn	Sonnenbrand
sun protection factor	Lichtschutzfaktor
sunscreen product	Sonnenschutzmittel
supper	Abendessen
supplement	Zusatz
supply	Versorgung
support	Unterstützung
suppository	Zäpfchen
surface	Oberfläche
surgeon	Chirurg
surgery	Praxis, Chirurgie
to survive	überleben
symptom	Symptom, Krankheitszeichen
syringe	Spritze
to swallow	schlucken
to sweat	schwitzen

T

table	Tabelle
to tan	bräunen
to tap	klopfen
tartar	Zahnstein
tartar scaling	Zahnsteinentfernung
task	Aufgabe
tax	Steuer
tea-mixture	Teemischung
teeth	Zähne
temporary filling	provisorische Füllung
tension	Spannung
term	Begriff
testis	Hoden
thermometer	Thermometer
thirsty	durstig
thorough	gründlich
throat	Rachen
thyme	Thymian
to tidy up	aufräumen
tights	Feinstrumpfhosen
time schedule	Terminkalender
tin	Zinn
tinted	getönt
tissue	Gewebe
toe	Zehe
tongue	Zunge
tool	Werkzeug
tooth	Zahn
toothache	Zahnschmerzen
toothbrush	Zahnbürste
toothpaste	Zahnpasta
topics	Themen
(to) touch	Berührung, berühren
towel	Handtuch
trade union	Gewerkschaft
trainee	Auszubildender
tranquilizer	Beruhigungsmittel
to translate	übersetzen
tray	Tablett
to treat	behandeln

treatment	Behandlung
treatment room	Behandlungsraum
to tremble	zittern
trouble	Probleme, Sorgen
true	wahr
to trust	vertrauen
truth	Wahrheit
turtle	Schildkröte
typical of	typisch für, charakteristisch für

U

ultrasound	Ultraschall
unconsciously	unbewußt
underneath	unterhalb
understanding	verständnisvoll
to undress	ausziehen
unfortunately	unglücklicherweise
to unwrap	auspacken
upper jaw	Oberkiefer
upset stomach	Magenverstimmung
ureter	Harnleiter
urethra	Harnröhre
urgent	dringend
urine	Urin
urologist	Urologe
to use	benutzen
usually	gewöhnlich, normalerweise
uterus	Gebärmutter

V

vacancy	offene Stelle
to vaccinate	impfen
vaccination	Impfung
vaccine	Impfstoff
vagina	Scheide
value	schätzen
to vary	variieren
various	verschieden
vein	Vene
veneer	Keramik Verblendschale
vertebrae	Wirbel
veterinarian, vet	Tierarzt
veterinarian's assistant	Tiermedizinische Fachangestellte
victim	Opfer
vital	lebensnotwendig
vocational school	Berufsschule
vocational training	Berufsausbildung
vomiting	Erbrechen

W

waiting-room	Wartezimmer
wall-picture	Wandzeitung
wardrobe	Kleiderschrank
wave	Welle
weak	schwach
weakness	Schwäche
to wear	tragen
to weigh	wiegen, abwiegen
well-organized	gut organisiert
wheelchair	Rollstuhl
whether	ob
white coat	Kittel
wholesaler	Großhändler
window display	Schaufensterauslage
windpipe	Luftröhre
wisdom tooth	Weisheitszahn
to withdraw	entziehen

(to) witness	Zeuge, bezeugen	**Y**	
to wonder	sich fragen		
working conditions	Arbeitsbedingungen	**yarrow**	Schafgarbe
workplace	Arbeitsplatz	**yolk**	Eigelb
worried	beunruhigt		
wound management	Wundversorgung	**Z**	
(to) wrinkle	Falte, faltig werden		
		zipper	Reißverschluss
X			
X-rays	Röntgenstrahlen		

Vocabulary German-English

A

Abendessen	supper
Abdruckmaterial	impression material
Abfallbehälter	bin
abgerundet	rounded
abhängen von	to depend on
abhängig von	dependent on
Abhängiger	addict
Abkommen	agreement
Ablehnung	rejection
ablenken (sich)	to distract oneself
abschwächen, verdünnen	to dilute
ähnlich	similar
ängstlich	frightened
Ärger	trouble
Ärmel	sleeves
äußern (sich) über	to comment on
Allergie	allergy
allgemein	general
Allgemeinmediziner	general practitioner
Alptraum	nightmare
Altenpflegerin, Altenpfleger	geriatric nurse
Alter	age
Altersheim	old people's home
ambulante Behandlung	outpatient treatment/service
ambulanter Pflegedienst	home care team
Anamese, Krankheits-vorgeschichte	medical history
Anamesebogen	medical history form
anbieten	to offer
anerkannt, gebilligt	approved
Angelegenheit, Problem	issue
angreifen	to attack
Angriff	attack
Angst	anxiety
anklagend	accusatory
anleiten, unterweisen	to instruct
Anmeldung	reception
anreichen (Instrumente)	to hand (instruments)
anrufen	to phone
Anstieg	increase, rise
Antikörper	antibody
antiretrovirale Therapie	antiretroviral therapy
Anweisung	instruction
anwenden	to apply
Anwendung	application
Apotheke	pharmacy
Apotheker	chemist, pharmacist
Arbeitgeber	employer
Arbeitsbedingungen	working conditions
Arbeitsplatz	workplace
Armut	poverty
Art (Zucht, Rasse)	breed
Arterie	artery
Artikel, Gegenstand	item
Arzt	doctor, physician
Arzneimittelallergie	drug allergy
Aschenbecher	ashtray
assistieren	to assist
assoziieren	to associate
Atem	breath
atmen	to breathe
Atmung	breathing
Atmungssystem	respiratory system
aufdringlich	pushy
Auffrischungsimpfung	booster injection
auffüllen	to stock up on
Aufgabe	task
aufgeschlossen	open-minded
Aufmerksamkeit	attention
aufräumen	to tidy up
aufregend	exciting
Aufregung	agitation
aufziehen (erziehen)	to bring up
Auge	eye
Augenarzt	ophthalmologist
ausbreiten	to spread
Ausdruck	expression
ausdrucken	to print out
ausdrücken	to squeeze
ausführen	to conduct
ausfüllen	to fill in
auslegen	to display
Ausnahme	exemption
auspacken	to unwrap
Ausschlag	rash
außer	except
außerdem	moreover
Aussichten	prospects
ausstellen	to exhibit
auswählen	to choose, to select
ausziehen	to undress
Auswahl	choice
Auszubildende	apprentice, trainee

B

Backenzahn, Molar	molar
Bakterium	bacterium
Bandbreite, Angebot	range
Bauch	stomach, belly
Bauchspeicheldrüse	pancreas
bedecken	to cover
bedienen	to serve
beeinflussen	to affect
Begriff	term
begründen	to explain
behandeln	to treat
Behandlung	treatment
Behandlungsraum	treatment room
(zahnärztlicher) Behand-lungsstuhl	(dental) chair
behindert	disabled
Behinderte	handicapped people
beinhalten	to contain, to include
belasten	to charge
Belastung	strain, burden
bemerken	to notice
benötigen, brauchen	to need
benutzen	to use
bequem	comfortable
Berechnung	calculation
berechtigt sein	to be eligible
Bericht	report
Berührung, berühren	touch, to touch
Beruf	profession, job, occupation

Berufsausbildung	vocational training
Berufskrankheit	occupational disease
Berufsschule	vocational school
beruhigen	to soothe
Beruhigungsmittel	sedative
beschädigt	damaged
Beschäftigte	employees
beschäftigen, einstellen	to employ
Beschäftigung	employment
Beschäftigungstherapie	occupational therapy
Bescheinigung	certificate
beschreiben	to describe
beschweren (sich)	to complain
Besitzer	owner
besonders	especially
besorgt	anxious
bestehen aus	to consist of
Bestellung	order
bestellen, anordnen	to order
betäuben	to anaesthetize
Betonung	emphasis
Betrag	amount
betreffend	concerning, according to
Bettjäckchen	bed jacket
Bettlaken	sheet
Bettzeug	bedclothes
beunruhigt	anxious, worried
Beurteilung, Bewertung	assessment
Bevölkerung	population
bevorzugen	to prefer
bewältigen	to manage
Beweis	proof
beweisen	to prove
bewerben um (sich)	to apply for
Bewerbung	application
Bewohner, Bewohnerin	resident
bewusst	conscious
bezeugen	to witness
Beziehung	relationship
bezüglich	concerning
Blase	bladder
Bleichen (von Zähnen)	bleaching
Blumenkohl	cauliflower
Blut	blood
Blutbild	blood picture
Blutdruck	blood pressure
Bluter	hemophiliac
Blutgefäß	blood vessel
Blutgerinnsel	clot
Blutzuckertest	blood sugar test
bösartig	malignant
Borste	bristle
Botengänge machen	to run errands
Botschaft, Nachricht	message
bräunen	to tan
Brennessel	stinging nettle
Brille, Brillengläser	glasses, spectacles
Bronchitis	bronchitis
Brosche	brooch
Brücke	bridge
Brust	breast
Brustkorb	chest
Buchstabe	letter
buchstabieren	to spell
Bürger, Bürgerin	citizen
Büroarbeit	office work
Büstenhalter	bra

C

Chirurg	surgeon
Chirurgie, Praxis	surgery
Cholesterinwert im Blut	blood cholesterol level

D

Dampf	steam
Dauerleihgabe	durable equipment
Decke	blanket
Demenz	dementia
deprimiert sein	to be blue
Desinfektion	disinfection
Diabetiker	diabetic
Diät	diet
Dialog	dialogue
Dokumentation	documentation
dringend	urgent
Droge, Medikament	drug
Druck	pressure/strain
Drüse	gland
Durchfall	diarrhoea
durchführen	to conduct
durchstellen (jmd.)	to put sb. through
durstig	thirsty
Dusche	shower

E

Eckzahn (Caninus)	canine
ehrlich	honest
Eierstock	ovary
Eigelb	yolk
Eileiter	fallopian tube
Eindringling	invader
Eindruck	impression
einführen	to introduce
eingeklemmt, impaktiert	impacted
Eingeweide	intestines
Einlagefüllung	inlay
Einrichtung	facility
Einsamkeit	loneliness
einsammeln	to collect
Einspritzung, Injektion	injection
einstellen, beschäftigen	to employ
Einstellung, Haltung	attitude
Einzelarbeit	individual work
Eisen	iron
EKG-Raum	electrocardiography
Elend	misery
Ellenbogen	elbow
empfehlen	to recommend, to advise
Empfehlung	advice
empfindlich	sensitive
Endodontie	endodontics
Entdeckung	discovery
entfernen	to eliminate, to remove
enthalten	to contain
enthüllen	to reveal
entscheiden	to decide
Entscheidung	decision
entspannen	to relax
entwickeln	to develop, to process, to devise
entziehen	to withdraw
(totale) Entziehung	cold-turkey
entzündet	inflamed
Entzug	deprivation
Erbrechen, sich übergeben	vomiting, to vomit
Erbsen	peas
Erde	soil, earth
erfahren	to experience
Erfahrung	experience
erfinden	to invent
erfolgreich	successful
Ergänzung	supplement
Ergebnis	result
Erinnerung	memory

Erleichterung	relief
Erfolg	success
erfrischen	to refresh
erhalten, pflegen	to maintain
erhalten, bekommen	to receive
erhöhen, vergrößern	to enhance
erholen (sich)	to recover
Erkältung	cold
erleichtern, lindern	to ease
Ernährung	diet, nutrition
ernst, ernsthaft	serious
erscheinen	to appear
Ersatz	substitute
erschöpft	exhausted
ersetzen	to replace
ertragen	to bear, to endure
erwähnen	to mention
erwarten	to expect
erziehen	to bring up
Essen auf Rädern	meals on wheels
Essraum	dining-room
Extraktionszange	extraction forceps

F

falsch	false
Familienstand	marital status
Fehler	fault
Feinstrumpfhosen	tights
Fenchel	fennel
Fertigkeit, Kenntnis	skill
fest	firm
feucht	damp
Feuchtigkeit	moisture
Fieber	fever
fiebrig	feverish
Fleck	stain
Fledermaus	bat
formen	to shape
Flyer	leaflet
fördern	to promote
Fragebogen	questionnaire
Frauenarzt	gynaecologist
freie Stelle	vacancy
freisetzen	to release
freiverkäufliches Präparat	over-the-counter-medicine
Frequenz	frequency
Frettchen	ferret
Frieden	peace
fröhlich	cheerful
Frontzahn	front tooth
Früherkennung	early detection
Frühschicht	morning shift
Füllungsmaterial	filling material
füttern	to feed
Funktionen	functions
Furcht	fear

G

Gallenblase	gall bladder
Gallensaft	bile
Gastroenterologe	gastroenterologist
Gebärmutter	uterus
Gebärmutterhals	cervics
Gebärmutterhalskrebs	cervical cancer
Gebühr	charge, fee
Gedicht	poem
Geduld	patience
Gefährte	companion
Gefühle	emotions
gegenseitig	mutual
Gegenstand, Artikel	item

Gehaltserhöhung	rise in salary
gehetzt	hurriedly
Gehirn	brain
Gehirnzellen	brain cells
gehören zu	to belong to
Geist, Gedächtnis	mind
Geldbörse	purse
Gelegenheit	opportunity, chance
gelegentlich	occasionally
genauso	likewise
Genesung	recuperation
genießen	to enjoy
Gericht, Speise	dish
geringfügig	minor
Geruch	scent, smell
Geschenk	gift
Geschwindigkeit	pace
Gesellschaft	society
Gesten	gestures
gesund	healthy
Gesundheit	health
getönt	tinted
Gewalt, Kraft	force
gewaltig, riesig	huge
Gewebe	tissue
Gewerkschaft	trade union
gewöhnlich, normalerweise	usuallly, common
Gift	poison
Grippe	influenza, flu
Großhändler	wholesaler
grübeln	to ruminate
gründlich	thorough
Grundinstrumente	basic instruments
Gummihandschuhe	rubber gloves
Gurke	cucumber

H

Hämatologe	haematologist
häufig	frequent
Hals	neck
Hals-Nasen-Ohren-Arzt	ENT specialist
Halsschmerzen	sore throat
Handlung	action
Handtuch	towel
Handverkaufstisch	counter
Harnleiter	ureter
Harnröhre	urethra
Haustier	pet
Haut	skin
Hautpflege	skincare
Hautarzt	dermatologist
heilbar	curable
heilen	to cure, to heal
Heilmittel	remedy
Heilung	cure
heimlich	secret
helle Haut	fair skin
herausfordernd	challenging
Herz	heart
Herzanfall, Herzinfarkt	heart attack
hinzufügen	to add
hören	to hear
Hörgerät	hearing aids
Hoden	testis
Hormonsystem	endocrine system
Huflattich	coltsfood
Husten	cough
Hustenbonbons	cough sweets
Hustensirup	cough syrup
Hustentee	cough tea
Hustentropfen	cough drops
Hypnose	hypnosis

I

impfen	to vaccinate
Impfstoff	vaccine
Impfung	vaccination
Immunsystem	immune system
impaktiert, eingeklemmt	impacted
Infektionskrankheit	infectious disease
Inhalt	contents
Injektion, Einspritzung	injection
injizieren	to inject
insbesondere	especially
Instrumente anreichen	to hand instruments
Internetrecherche	Internet Research
intravenös	intravenous

J

jenseits (von)	beyond
juckend	itchy

K

Kamille	camomile
Kamm	comb
Kaninchen	rabbit
Kardiologe	cardiologist
Karies	caries
Karteikarte	file card, medical record
Karteikasten	file card box
Kartoffelbrei	mashed potatoes
Kaufläche	biting surface
Kavität (Loch im Zahn)	cavity
Kerl, Typ	guy
Kette	chain
Kieferorthopädie	orthodontics
Kinderarzt	paediatrician
Kinderhort, Kinderkrippe	day nursery
Kittel	white coat
Klammer	brace
Klammern	parentheses
Klassenkameraden	classmates
Kleiderschrank	wardrobe
Kleinstlebewesen	microorganism
kleiner Backenzahn	pre-molar
klopfen	to tap
Knochen	bone
Knorpel	cartilage
Körper	body
Körperhaltung	posture
körperlich	physical
körperliche Anstrengung	physical exertion
körperliche Kraft	physical strength
Körpersprache	body language
Kohlenhydrate	carbohydrates
Kollege	colleague
konservierende Zahn- heilkunde	restorative dentistry
Kontaktlinsen	contact lenses
Kopf	head
Kopfschmerz	headache
Koronararterie	coronar artery
kräftigen, stärken	to strengthen
Kraft, Gewalt	force
krank	ill, sick
Krankengymnast	physical therapist
Krankenhaus	hospital
Krankenversicherung	health insurance
Krankenvericherungskarte	medical card
Krankheit	disease, illness
Krebs	cancer
kreisförmig	circular
Kreislaufsystem	circulatory system
Krone	crown
Kühlschrank	refrigerator
(sich) kümmern um	to care for
kürzlich	recently
Kunde	customer
Kundenzeitschrift	customer magazine
Kunststoff-Füllung	composite filling

L

Lähmung	paralysis
launisch, mürrisch	moody
Lebenslauf	curriculum vitae
Lebensmittel	food
Lebensmittelallergie	food allergy
Lebensmittelvergiftung	food poisoning
Lehrling	apprentice
leiden unter	to suffer from
leisten (sich)	to afford
Lichtschutzfaktor	sun protection factor
liefern, bieten	to provide
lindern, erleichtern	to ease
Loch im Zahn	cavity
lösen (Problem)	to solve
(etwas) loswerden	to get rid of something
Lücke	gap, blank
Luftröhre	windpipe
Luftverschmutzung	air pollution
Lungenentzündung	pneumonia

M

männliche Geschlechts- organe	male reproductive system
Magen	stomach
Magen-Darm-Grippe	gastric flu
Magenverstimmung	upset stomach
Magersucht	anorexia nervosa
Mastdarm	rectum
Medikament, Droge	drug
medizinische Erstbehandlung, -versorgung	primary medical care
Medizinische Fachangestellte	doctor's assistant
Medizinisches Wörterbuch	medical dictionary
Meerschweinchen	guinea pig
Mehrwertsteuer	V.A.T. (value added tax)
Mensch	human being
messen	to measure
mildern, erleichtern	to relieve
Minderheit	miority
minderwertig	inferior
Missbrauch	abuse
Mittagessen	lunch
Möhren	carrots
Mullbinde	gauze bandage
Mund	mouth
Munddusche	mouth rinse
Mundwasser	mouthwash
Muskel	muscle
Muskelschmerz	muscle pain
Muster	pattern
Muttermal, Leberfleck	mole

N

nach	post
Nachfrage	demand
Nachthemd	night-dress
Nachtschränkchen	bedside table
Nährcreme	nourishing creme
Nährstoff	nutrient

Nagelschere	nail scissors	Rasse (Art)	breed
Nase	nose	Ratschlag	advice
Nebenwirkung	side effect	rauh	rough
Neffe	nephew	reagieren auf	to respond to
Nervenenden	nerve endings	Rechnung	bill, invoice
Nervensystem	nervous system	Regal	shelf
Nervenarzt	neurologist	Regierung	government
niesen	to sneeze	registrieren	to register
Notfall	emergency	Reihenuntersuchung	screening
notwendig	necessary	reinigen	to purify, to clean
Nudelgericht	pasta	Reißverschluss	zipper
Nutzen	benefit	reizen	to irritate
		Reptil	reptile
O		Reserviertheit	aloofness
ob	whether	retten	to save, to rescue
Oberfläche	surface	Rezept	prescription
Oberkiefer	upper jaw	riesig, gewaltig	huge
Oberkörper freimachen	to strip to the waist	Risikopatient	high-risk patient
obwohl	although	Rippe	rib
öffentlicher Gesundheits- dienst	public health service	Rock	skirt
		Röntgenstrahl	X-ray
OHP-Folie	overhead transparency	röntgen	to X-ray
Orthopädie	orthopaedist	Röteln	rubella
örtlich	local	rollen	to scroll
Östrogen	estrogen	Rollstuhl	wheelchair
Opfer	victim	Rücken	back
Optiker	optician, optometrist		
Ohr	ear	**S**	
Ohrstück	earpiece	Salbe	ointment
		Salbei	sage
P		sammeln	to collect
Papiertaschentücher	paper tissues	Säure	acid
Parodontalbehandlung	periodontics	Sauerstoff	oxygen
Partnerarbeit	pair work	Schachtelhalm	horsetail
Patient	patient	Schaden	damage
Pause	break	schaden	to damage
Pauschale	flat charge	Schädel	skull
Penis	penis	schätzen	to value
Pensionierung	retirement	Schafgarbe	yarrow
Personalien	personal data	Schal	scarf
Personalraum,-garderobe	staff cloakroom	Schallwelle	sound wave
Pfefferminze	peppermint	Schaufensterauslage	window display
Pflegeheim für ältere Personen	elder care center	Schauspieler	actor
		Scheide	vagina
pflegerisch	custodial	Scheidung	divorce
Pickel	spot	Schildkröte	turtle
Pilz	fungus	Schläfchen	nap
plagen	to bother	Schlaflosigkeit	sleeplessness
plaudern	to chat	Schlaganfall	stroke
Pocken	smallpox	schlank	slim
Präsentationsaufgabe	presentation task	schlucken	to swallow
Praxis	surgery	Schlüsselbein	collar bone
Präkanzerös	pre-cancerous Problem,	Schlüsselqualifikationen	key qualifications
Angelegenheit	problem, issue	Schmerz	pain, ache
Prospekt	leaflet	schmerzen	to ache, to hurt
Prothetik	prosthetics	schmerzhaft	painful
Prothesen	prostheses	schmerzlos	painless
provisorische Füllung	temporary filling	Schmerzmittel	painkiller
Prüfung, Untersuchung	examination	schneiden	to cut
Psychiater	psychiatrist	Schneidezahn	incisor
Psychologe	psychologist	schrecklich	awful, terrible
Pullover	jumper	schrubben, scheuern	to scrub
		Schublade	drawer
Q		Schulter	shoulder
quälen	to bother	Schutz	protection
		schützen vor	to protect from
R		schwach	weak
Rachen	throat	Schwäche	weakness
Radiologe	radiologist	schwanger	pregnant
		Schwangerschaft	pregnancy
		Schweiß	sweat
		schwierig (herausfordernd)	challenging

VOCABULARY

schwindelig	dizzy
Seife (Stück)	bar of soap
Seitenzahn	side tooth
Selbstachtung	self-esteem
seltsam	strange
Skelett	skeleton
skizzieren	to sketch
Sodbrennen	heartburn
Sonde	probe
Sonnenbrand	sunburn
Sonnenschutzmittel	sunscreen protection
sorgen für	to care for
sorgfältig	careful
Sozialhilfe	social security
Spalte	column
Spannung	tension
Speichel	saliva
Speise, Gericht	dish
Spiegel	mirror
spiegeln	to mirror
Sprechstundenzeiten	consulting hours
Sprechzimmer	consulting room
Spritze	syringe
stark	severe
stechend	piercing
stempeln	to stamp
sterben	to die
Sterilisation	sterilization
Stimmung	mood
Stirn	forehead
Streit, Auseinandersetzung	quarrel
Steuer	tax
suchen nach	to search for
Suchmaschine	search engine
Süchtiger	addict
Symptom	symptom

T

Tabelle	table, chart
Tablett	tray
tapfer	brave
Teemischung	tea-mixture
Telefongespräch	phone call
Telefonhörer	receiver
teilen	to share
Termin	appointment
Terminkalender	time schedule
Thema	topic
Thymian	thyme
Tier	animal
Tierarzt	veterinarian, vet
Tiermedizinische Fachangestellte	veterinarian's assistant
Tod	death
Todesurteil	death sentence
Tollwut	rabies
tragen	to wear
treu	faithful
Typ, Kerl	guy
typisch für	typical of

U

Übelkeit, Brechreiz	nausea
überbeschützend	overprotective
Überdosis	overdose
überleben	to survive
über . . . hinaus	beyond
überprüfen	to check
übersetzen	to translate
Überstunden	overtime
übertragen	to pass

überweisen	to refer
Überweisung	referral
überzeugen	to convince
Ultraschall	ultrasound
Umgebung, Umwelt	environment
Unabhängig	independent
unbewusst	unconscious
Unfähigkeit	inability
Unfall	accident
ungeachtet	regardless
unglücklicherweise	unfortunately
unsichtbar	invisible
unterhalb	underneath
unterhalten (sich)	to chat
Unterhaltung	conversation
Unterstützung	support
untersuchen	to examine, to check
(gründliche) Untersuchung	check-up
Untersuchungsliege	examination couch
(sich) unterscheiden von	to differ from
unterweisen, anleiten	to instruct
unzufrieden	dissatisfied
Urologe	urologist
Ursache	cause

V

variieren	to vary
Vene	vein
Veränderung	change
verantwortungsbewusst	responsible
Verantwortungsbewusstsein	responsibility
Verband	bandage
verbessern	to improve
verbinden (mit)	to associate
Verbindung, Verweis	link
verdauen	to digest
Verdauung	digestion
Verdauungssystem	digestive system
Verdienstmöglichkeiten	earnings
verdünnen, abschwächen	to dilute
Verfallsdatum	best-before date
verfügbar	available
Vergangenheit	past
vergleichen	to compare
Verhalten	behaviour
Verhaltensweise	manner
Verlangen nach	craving for
verlegen, peinlich berührt	embarrassed
Verletzung	injury
vermeiden	to avoid
vermindern	to reduce
vernachlässigen	to neglect
verringern	to lower
Versagen	failure
verschlimmern	to aggravate
verschreiben	to prescribe
verschwinden	to disappear
verseucht	contaminated
versprechen	to promise
versichern	to insure
Versicherungsprämie	premium
Versicherungsschutz	coverage
Versiegeler	dental sealant
versorgen	to supply
Versorgung	supply
verständnisvoll	understanding
verstecken	to hide
Verstopfung	constipation
verteidigen gegen	to defend against
Verteidigung	defence
verteilen	to distribute
vertrauen	to trust

verursachen	to cause
vervollständigen	to complete
Verwaltung	administration
verwirrt	confused
voranschreiten	to progress
vorbereiten	to prepare
Vorbeugung	prevention
vorbeugen, verhindern	to prevent
vorhergehend	previous
Vorliebe	like
Vorname	forename
vorschlagen	to suggest
Vorsichtsmaßnahme	precaution
(sich etwas) vorstellen	to imagine
(jdn) vorstellen	to introduce sb
Vorteil	advantage

W

Wachstum	growth
während	during
Wahl (Auswahl)	choice
wahr	true
Wahrheit	truth
wandern	to hike
Wandzeitung	wall-picture, wall-paper
Wange	cheek
Warensendung	delivery
Wartezimmer	waiting room
Wasserstoffsuperoxid	hydrogen peroxide
Wattestäbchen	cotton bud
weder . . . noch	neither . . . nor
wegwerfbar	disposable
Welle	wave
weiblich	female
weibliche Geschlechts-organe	female reproductive system
Weisheitszahn	wisdom tooth
Werkzeug	tool
widersprüchlich	contradictory
widerstandsfähig gegen	resistant to
wiederholen	to repeat
wiegen	to weigh
Winkel	angle
Wirbel	vertebrae
Wirbelsäule	spine
Wohnort	place of residence
Wundversorgung	wound management
Wurzel	root
Wurzelkanal	root canal
Wurmfortsatz	appendix
Wut	anger

Z

Zäpfchen	suppository
Zahlungsverpflichtung	payment obligation
Zahn, Zähne	tooth, teeth
Zahnarzt	dentist
Zahnarztpraxis	dental surgery
Zahnbein	dentine
Zahnbelag	plaque
Zahnbürste	toothbrush
Zahnfleisch	gum
Zahnfleischentzündung	gingivitis
Zahnfleischerkrankung	gum disease
Zahnfleischrand	gum margin
Zahnfäule	decay
Zahnmark	pulp
Zahnmedizinische Fachangestelte	dental assistant
Zahnmedizinisches Wörterbuch	dental dictionary
Zahnpasta	toothpaste
Zahnprothese	dental plate
Zahnschmerzen	toothache
Zahnschmelz	enamel
Zahnstein	tartar
Zahnsteinentfernung	tartar scaling
Zahnseide	dental floss
Zahntechniker	dental technician
Zahnzwischenraumbürste	interproximal brush
Zehe	toe
zeichnen	to draw
Zelle	cell
Zeitschrift	magazine
Zement	cement
zerstören	to destroy
zerstörerisch	destructive
zerren, reißen	to tear
Zeugnis	certificate, reference
zittern	to tremble, to shiver
zögern	to hesitate
Zorn	anger
zubereiten, vorbereiten	to prepare
Zucht (Rasse, Art)	breed
Zuckerkrankheit	diabetes
Zugang	access
Zuneigung	affection
Zunge	tongue
Zutritt	admittance
Zweck	purpose
zwingen	to force
Zytostatika	cytotoxic drugs